THE Course is conducted by Mr. F. Matthias Alexander and his Assistant Teachers at 16 Ashley Place, London, S.W.1. Its purpose is to train students to impart the technique set down in his books, "Man's Supreme Inheritance," "Constructive Conscious Control of the Individual," "The Use of the Self" and "The Universal Constant in Living." (More detailed information is given in "Open Letter to Intending Students of Training Course," which is printed as an Appendix to "The Use of the Self," published in 1932.)

Both men and women are required for training as teachers, but they should not be less than 18 years of age, or more than 35, at the commencement of the Course. No special educational qualifications are demanded, but a prospective student must satisfy Mr. F. Matthias Alexander personally that he, or she, possesses the character, outlook, and general qualities that should make for a successful teacher of his technique. To this end it is recommended that a student should receive some private lessons in the technique before entering the Training Course, but this is not essential in all cases.

The normal duration of the Training Course is three years; and each year is divided into two Sessions, from about September 10th. to November 30th., and about January 20th., to July 20th. In certain cases, however, a fourth year of training is required. Candidates who are accepted by Mr. Alexander may arrange to start their Course at any time.

Walter Carrington

A Time To Remember

By the same author:
The F. Matthias Alexander Technique – A Means of
Understanding Man (booklet)
Man's Future as an Individual (booklet)
Balance as a Function of Intelligence (booklet)
Walter Carrington on the Alexander Technique (with Seán Carey)
Explaining the Alexander Technique (with Seán Carey)
Thinking Aloud (ed. J. Sontag)
The Foundations of Human Well-Being & The Work of Professor
Magnus and the F. Matthias Alexander Technique

Walter H. M. Carrington

A Time To Remember

A Personal Diary of Teaching the F. M. Alexander Technique in 1946

With notes by Jean M. O. Fischer

The Sheildrake Press

First published 1996

The Sheildrake Press
18 Lansdowne Road
London W11 3LL
England

ISBN 0–9519998–1–8 hardback

British Library Cataloguing-in-Publication Data
A catalogue record for this book is available from
the British Library.

Design and layout by Jean M. O. Fischer.
Set in Monotype Bembo 12/14 in Aldus
PageMaker 5.0. Printed on 90gsm BookWove
and bound by The Bath Press, Bath

The endpapers show a facsimile of the prospectus
for F. Matthias Alexander's Training Course, 1946

CONTENTS

PREFACE

I have never been in the habit of keeping a diary, but when I
returned from my service in the R.A.F., in March 1946, I realized
that I was opening a new chapter in my life, or rather, reopening
an old one. It seemed that the next few months were likely to
prove momentous for me, and so I started to make a brief record
of events.

A diary is a very personal affair, usually intended only for
oneself, not to be read by others. It may be trivial, indiscreet,
injudicious and ephemeral; and yet convey a vivid impression, a
sense of the fleeting moment so easily lost and forgotten. To
publish such a record may risk offence to both living and dead
where none was intended, or convey opinions or judgements
that are false in hindsight. However, today there is so much interest in the history of the Alexander Technique, so many people
would like to know more about FM himself, and what the training course was like when he was running it, that I have decided
to take this risk and publish the diary much as it was written,
with only a few alterations and amendments for the sake of clar-
ity and to avoid gratuitous pain to people still alive.

It gives some impression of what life was like for us all immediately after the war. In 1946 we were slowly picking up the
threads from 1939 and looking towards the future. So far as the
work was concerned, it was a quiet year and the training course
was much as it had always been. Only towards the end did the
shadow of the South African Libel Action began to fall, distract-
ing so much of our time and energy and disrupting all our future
plans. It was in the following summer that the case commenced
with the taking of evidence on Commission, and it was at that
Christmas that FM had his stroke. Thereafter, although he resumed his work with the students, and continued with his private teaching, the course was never quite the same.

I had finished my training and gained my Teaching Certificate in July 1939, and I had continued to work at Ashley Place
until March 1941, when I commenced my service in the R.A.F.

I was trained as a pilot and in 1944 my crew and I were shot down over Hungary and I sustained a fractured pelvis, jaw, and collar-bone and sundry lesser injuries. We were all taken prisoner but I was moved to a military hospital in Szeged from which I eventually escaped by help of the local Jesuit Fathers. The Russian Army captured the town where I was lodged in the Jesuit College, and the Russians flew me back to Bucharest and handed me over to our British Military Mission. Eventually I returned to England and resumed my flying duties in which I continued until after the war.

During this long interlude I was constantly putting to the test what I had learned of the Alexander Technique. It proved an invaluable resource in learning new skills, such as flying an aircraft, and in coping generally with the unfamiliar and the unknown. Of course I longed for the day when the war would be over and I should be able to return to Alexander and to my work as an Assistant Teacher but I knew that I should need a lot of help, a lot of retraining, before I could be fit to put hands on other people again. I got my discharge on Saturday 2nd March, and I was back in the training course at 11 o'clock on Monday 4th March.

Before continuing, I perhaps should describe N° 16 Ashley Place, the place so well remembered by Alexander's many pupils and students. It was near Victoria Station, towards the centre of a terrace of large Victorian stucco-faced houses, just behind Victoria Street and within sight of Westminster Cathedral. It appeared, from the outside, to be a three-storey, double-fronted house with its basement area railed off, and with coal-cellars below the pavement. A wide flight of steps led to a double front door. However, this appearance was deceptive. In fact the property was only a large apartment, consisting of a ground floor and a basement: there was no access from it to the floors above, which were entered from the adjoining houses.

FM had previously been living at 22 Army and Navy Mansions, Victoria Street, but as his work became more known, he needed more space and began to look for a place where he could both live and work. When he saw N° 16 Ashley Place, he knew that it would be ideal for his purposes. He was most anxious to secure it. It was about this time that he met Chiro, the celebrated palmist and clairvoyant. Chiro said he knew he was negotiating for new premises and predicted that he would be successful; however, Chiro was puzzled how to describe the property in question. He saw it as neither a house nor a flat, but as something of both. In fact, the property had been designed for Henry Labouchere, the well-known journalist and Member of Parliament who wanted a *pied á terre* near the House of Commons. With its large reception rooms and impressive private entrance, it provided the advantages of a house but with the convenience of a flat or an apartment. FM was overjoyed when he secured the lease.

To describe N° 16 from the point of view of a student on the training course: you approached the double front door and rang the bell. There was a small window or wicket let into the glass of the door on the right. By inserting a hand you could release the lock and so enter. On entry there was a small vestibule, another step, and you were in a rather dark entrance hall, with a dresser, on the right, convenient for leaving coats and hats. Straight ahead was a small waiting-room. FM's teaching room lay to the left, and behind it there was another room that served as an office. (Incidentally, the connecting door between these two rooms nearly always stood open, so anyone could look in and see and hear what was taking place in FM's room without causing disturbance or being observed.) A passage ran transversely in front of the waiting room door, leading to the left to the office, and to the right, to FM's cigar cupboard, of which he was very proud. (He maintained that it was the most perfect cupboard for the purpose, being in the centre of the building, protected from damp, but with a constant temperature. He was not a heavy smoker but he was a connoisseur of a fine cigar, which he often enjoyed after dinner in the evening. He also occasionally smoked a cigarette, as many people did in those days; but as far as I know, unlike his brother AR, he never smoked a pipe.)

Along this passage on the left was the door to a small back room used by the students, containing an upholstered couch and a set of large mirrors that could be adjusted to give a three-dimensional view of a person working in front of them. Next to this was the entry to a rather narrow twisting staircase leading to the basement. In the basement were the dining-room, FM's bedroom, the kitchen and the bathroom.

On the right of the passage were two doors close together: the first gave entry into what was known as the Students' Room, and the second into a further large room, known as AR's room, where FM's brother used to teach. This had also been used as the schoolroom before the Little School moved to Penhill. These two big reception rooms were divided from each other by curtained glass doors that could be drawn back, so as to make one large room.

It should be remembered that for years this was FM's home as well as his teaching establishment. He had furnished it with some handsome pieces of antique furniture, some fine pictures, and Persian rugs that it had been his great interest and pleasure to collect. The rooms were decorated in a style that was fashionable immediately after the Great War. The paintwork was black, the walls were a pale orange-yellow, as were the net curtains. The upholstery was mainly black or dark blue and there was parquet flooring throughout. The total effect was dark and warm but opulent.

In the 'Students' Room', as you entered, there was, on the left wall, a small chest of drawers and over it a picture by Wright of Derby, a study in candlelight. On the wall behind the door to the right, there was a portrait after Gainsborough and a Sheraton bookcase with a display of fine china. A black settee stood in front of the bookcase, at right-angles to the fireplace, facing the three triple sash-windows, looking out onto the street. In front of them was an oak bureau or escritoire. There was also a large black armchair in the corner by the window, with a black-framed mirror hanging over it.

This was the room that FM used as his drawing-room in the evenings and into which he took me the first time I met him in 1935. I remember sitting next to him on the settee beside a coal fire that blazed in the hearth, with its heavy dark over-mantel and gleaming fender with a copper coal-scuttle and brass fire-irons. In a further corner of the room was a tall corner cupboard from which he took a bottle of Tio Pepe and some handsome wineglasses.

Now this room was used mainly for the training course, but the furnishing remained unchanged, apart from the Sheraton bookcase that had perished when a bomb fell in a street close by and blew out all the windows. A few more stools and straight-backed chairs had also been provided for the use of the students. The room was available for them throughout the day, but FM's class was usually held either late in the morning or early in the afternoon. This was the time when he personally worked with the students.

When that time came, they would assemble, either standing or sitting round the room, more or less in a circle. FM would enter and begin straight away to work on the nearest student, then passing on to the next, and so on until he had completed the round, which he always seemed to manage by the end of the hour, whereupon he departed again. During this time, working on each individually, he would take some in and out of the chair, put some into 'monkey,' make others say 'whispered *ah*'s' or take them 'up on the toes'. Meanwhile, there would usually be some general conversation going on about any topic, sport, cricket, or the news of the day; or people might ask questions, and FM would reply and demonstrate some point (as can be seen from this diary). Very seldom did he invite anyone to work with their hands, but he would often get us to put hands on the back of a chair. Meanwhile, the assistant teachers would follow him round giving 'turns' successively as he had done. Students were expected to watch and observe and to work on themselves when they were not being worked on. FM regarded the students as his apprentices and saw the whole training as a form of old-fashioned apprenticeship. You were to learn from the master, to do what he asked (and to make yourself generally useful) but not to imitate him! It may be mentioned that he had no servants at this time but we all willingly ran errands for him and answered the telephone or opened the front door to newcomers who did not know the trick of letting themselves in.

After class was the time when students were expected to work on themselves, lying down on rugs on the floor with books under the head, or with hands on the back of the chair, sitting and coming forward from the hips, saying whispered *ah's*, or observing themselves in front of the mirrors in the back room. Senior students and assistant teachers might now offer 'turns' to each other and to the remainder of the class. They were not encouraged to put hands on each other until they had been in the training course for a considerable time, at least two years, and had FM's permission. (It should be recalled that the normal duration of the course was three years although most of the original students had done a fourth year to make up for all the time spent in the production of the plays, *The Merchant of Venice* and *Hamlet*. The course that started in 1945 also did four years on account of FM's absence whilst suffering from his stroke.)

As previously mentioned, FM had reinstituted the training course in the previous September, after the interruption of the war years. Now when I rejoined, the new course was nearing the end of its second term and the class numbered about fifteen. There were ten or eleven new students and a few who had not completed their training in 1940 when FM went to America. There were also several Assistant Teachers: Irene Stewart and Marjory Barlow, Pat Macdonald and Max Alexander and Margaret Goldie. Margaret, however, was usually teaching round the corner at her flat in Evelyn Mansions.

FM was now 77 years old, but just as slim and elegant as ever, with a bird-like energy and sprightliness. His hands were as gentle but compelling as before, and his direction seemed even more powerful. He was usually full of good humour and cheerfulness, but his keen observation of an individual's difficulties and shortcomings made him strict and precise in all his dealings. The war years might have taken their toll, but this was not evident.

He had gone to America in 1940 with great reluctance, taking with him the staff and children from the Little School at

Penhill. There he had finished and published his new book *The Universal Constant in Living*, whilst teaching in New York and Boston as well as starting a new teachers training course, with his brother, AR, in Stowe, Massachusetts, where the Little School had now settled. He was not happy to be away from England during those dark days. He was most anxious to return, and eventually he made the perilous journey home in 1943. In his absence, N⁰ 16 had suffered some bomb damage and he lost a few of his treasured possessions, but all was soon repaired, and he was able to resume his teaching practice. As for his beloved home, Penhill (near Bexley, Kent), that had largely escaped and he was able once more to enjoy the peace of his little estate and the fruits of his vegetable garden. Sadly, his old horse Peter had died in the meantime and so he could no longer have a ride as he used to do; which, as he used to say, 'does me so much good'.

Dilys and I had got married in 1940, shortly after FM went to America. During the time that I was away in the Air Force, she lived with her parents in Worcestershire, and we had two small boys. (Our third son was born later in 1947). As soon as the war was over, she returned to London and went to live in my father's vicarage, at St. Saviour's, Shepherd's Bush. It was to be our home for the next two years. I returned there to resume our pre-war existence and it is to there that many of the incidents in this diary refer.

Walter H. M. Carrington
London, April 1996

A Note on the Text

The diary has been reproduced in its entirety with the exception of a few sentences which Walter Carrington has deleted. Spelling mistakes have been corrected and some minor textual changes have been made, with regard to punctuation and capitalization for example. Explanatory additions appear in square brackets [ ].

The subject notes are intended to provide a brief introduction (or reminder as the case may be). Where specific reference is made to an event, situation or subject, the note is intended to elucidate and validate it. Subject notes are numbered and are placed before the biographical notes.

Biographical notes are in alphabetical order according to surname. The biographical notes focus on people of relevance to the narrative, e.g. teachers of the Alexander Technique, students, and other people who were involved in the furthering of the Technique at the time. Where relevant (and possible) I have mentioned where people were in their lives in or around 1946. It has not been possible to obtain information on all teachers and people who play a significant part in the diary. Where a biographical note exists the name is marked with an asterisk (*) where it first occurs.

Some of the abbreviations which appear are:

BMA	British Medical Association
BMJ	*British Medical Journal*
FRCS	Fellow of the Royal College of Surgeons
RNVR	Royal Navy Volunteer Reserve
STAT	The Society of Teachers of the Alexander Technique
WAAF	Women's Auxiliary Air Force
W/Cdr	Wing Commander

Abbreviations for F. M. Alexander's books are:

MSI	*Man's Supreme Inheritance*
CCC	*Constructive Conscious Control of the Individual*
UoS	*The Use of the Self*
UCL	*The Universal Constant in Living*

Any page reference to these refers to the 1946 editions.

ACKNOWLEDGEMENTS

For information for the notes I am indebted to Max Alexander, Kathleen Ballard, Marjory Barlow, Jevan Berrangé, Brian Campbell, Dilys Carrington, Walter Carrington, Chile Eagar, Erik Hellstenius, Mary Holland, David Morrison, Douglass Price-Williams, Duncan Stewart, Elisabeth Walker, Erika Whittaker, Miriam Wohl, and especially Yvonne Becker and Thea Kreft. In addition I owe many thanks to Ian MacFadyen for his critical examination of the contents of the notes and for correcting many grammatical mistakes. Any remaining mistakes in the notes are my responsibility.

I am grateful to Erika Whittaker for the use of her 1931 photo which appears on page 74. The pamphlets which are reproduced in facsimile are from Walter Carrington's archives.

Jean M. O. Fischer
London, April 1996

Monday 4th March

I was released from the Air Force on Saturday but my 'effective date of release' is not until May 10th. Until then I am paid at full rates and allowances. Yesterday I had lunch with Haynes* and drank champagne again – almost the only wine he can get. Today I returned to Ashley Place to re-enter the students' training course after an interval of five and a half years. It was in August 1939 that I qualified as a teacher. Dick Walker* was there today. He is still in the Navy but on indefinite leave. Bill Barlow* is more or less in the same position with regard to his medical work for the Army. Alma Frank* came in. She arrived this morning by plane from America and is staying with the Barlows. FM was in great form but he is showing signs of age now. His teaching is better than ever though! Pat's [Macdonald*] hands are very good. Irene Stewart* seems excellent too. Marjory Barlow* gave me a short turn also. She has improved a lot but perhaps is not quite so deft as Pat. They have all improved out of all knowledge since before the war.

FM spoke of the reliability of expert judgement and the errors that experts make. He instanced Dr Johnson's condemnation of Hamlet's 'To be or not to be' speech[1] and another critic's rejection of Keats' *Endymion;* the latter was advised to return to his pestle and mortar.[2] Later FM spoke with approval of Attlee's dull and insipid speech on the wireless last night.[3] He considered it excellent! Would this be another instance of expert opinion, or is it my judgement that is at fault?

Tuesday 5th March

I worked with the students this morning, first of all lying on the floor. The difficulty of disentangling thinking and feeling was paramount as usual and I was amused to note how difficult it was to make any movement of head or limbs without prejudicing the 'total pattern'. There is a lot of ground to recover here.

The question of conception was raised – the old one of Alma's – whether it helps to know what the back is from an anatomical point of view when giving orders. Dr Dorothy Drew [Morrison*] said not: she added that, whereas knowledge of 'the work' contributes to anatomy, a knowledge of anatomy is, if anything, a hindrance to the pupil. She instanced her own early attempts to direct the sub-occipital muscles directly until 'straight-ened' by Bill.

In the afternoon Speransky was mentioned and Alma said that she had brought his book[4] over with her in 1937 and twice sent copies of the three books to him in Russia. She does not know if he ever got them and never received any acknowledge-ment. I had entirely forgotten this incident until reminded of it.

FM can now get what he wants with his hands with the barest touch. The others are good and can get it but tend to 'do' too much, thus inclining to over-stimulate. An amusing incident occurred when, being called to the telephone, I utterly failed to inhibit the stimulus to get up and had three shots at it with FM's very delicate help before I could respond properly. FM remarked that it is the good people who do all the harm in the world. This fits into the argument that I have been developing for some time past. The supposedly good people are those who use reason, with some greater or lesser degree of success, to make changes in habit and environment. The others are generally content to live in a static environment according to fixed habit. But it is change brought about by imperfect procedures based on incomplete premises that causes most of the trouble in the world.

Wednesday 6th March

Today was Pat's birthday: Dilys [Carrington*] and I gave him *Gargantua and Pantagruel*, a new abridgement of Rabelais. He seemed pleased. It was bitterly cold and my back has started to ache again. I had lunch with Mother at Dickens & Jones, after which there was an uneventful class. I'm improving gradually but am full of misgivings. Have we got a chance of getting to where

FM has got to without imitating his experiences? And how is this to be done without his motivation and driving force?

Mungo Douglas* has done an excellent paper on Speransky, according to FM. I returned home immediately after the class.

Thursday 7th March

I had lunch with Olive Gaze today in Symonds Restaurant. We had a very nice chat but not a very good lunch. AR [Alexander*] came into the students' class this afternoon, looking surprisingly well. I was more 'up' and less tired. Bill asked one of Robert Best's* favourite questions: 'Is "use" synonymous with "reaction"?' FM said that it was.

Later I had tea with Dick Walker at the Stores. He and I were stationed only a few miles from each other in Italy, it seems, for he was operating in the Adriatic all the time. We talked of many aspects of the work and the proposed Institute.[5] It surprises me that students are not more familiar with the books.[6]

Friday 8th March

The students' class was held in the morning and FM was in particularly good form. Talking of an editor who had not seen the connection between interim discoveries described in his paper and the Technique, he said that it did not surprise him that people failed to make this connection. They had never conceived of anything of the nature of a Primary Control. All their thought was based on a principle of separation. In answer to a query he replied that he had never found any limit to the depths of human stupidity.

One of the students remarked that she had thought herself doing badly yesterday and well today. FM said that quite the reverse of this was the case. He had long ago given up asking people how they were doing, or telling them that they were doing well, because he found it had such a bad effect on them. He said that he had never yet had anybody come to him and say that they had mastered the secret of the Technique who was not quite wrong. When people work on themselves in front of a mirror and see their necks free and that they do not pull back their heads when they sit down, for example, they are very pleased. But it is not the 'head going forward and up' that counts, it is what happens to the back at the same time. If anyone says they have seen wonderful changes in lengthening and widening the back they are sure to be wrong, because when the proper conditions are present there is nothing to see. The head going forward and up checks the back lengthening and widening, and the back the head. That is why the work is so simple and you cannot go wrong in teaching if you observe these conditions. The change that takes place is a process of growth and is not to be observed instantaneously. Experts always want to see some specific changes brought about by the Technique. FM was once offered a room at Guy's because the head of the orthopaedic department there said that they wanted to watch some specific changes being made. So that if it was satisfactory FM might be asked to work there permanently. But this proposition was referred to J. E. R. McDonagh* and, at a dinner party, he and FM convinced the specialist concerned that he would see nothing in such circumstances.

FM said that when he first started to teach he was told by the medical men that sent patients to him that he must take care to remember what was wrong with each of the patients. He soon saw that this was a fundamentally unsound outlook for it leads one to approach the pupil with a prejudiced mind and a preconceived idea. He said it had taken him about three years to acquire the habit of never remembering one day what the pupil's condition had been on the previous day.

After this interesting class I had an excellent lunch with Pat and Dorothy Drew at our little pub; and then did a quiet afternoon's work in the students' room.

Monday 11th March
On Saturday we took the children to Pat's for a lesson and Sunday was Richard's birthday. The latter was a perfect day for the children and Richard was thrilled by his new scooter and by his birthday cake which Dilys had iced in the shape of a house.

Today in the class Bill asked FM if he thought that conscious direction could stop bleeding. FM replied that this was certainly so with regard to haemorrhage of the lungs. One of the first cases that a doctor sent to him in Australia was of this nature and it stopped in a few lessons and never recurred. In 1904 when he first came to England a medical man had written a large book on haemorrhage arguing that if you cut your finger the flow of blood would soon stop but in the lung there was no means of stopping it, the difference being that you could keep the finger still and not move it whereas with the lung this was impossible. He therefore advocated that the chest should be very tightly strapped up in these cases to reduce movement to a minimum. FM described this theory to Spicer* as lunacy, saying that if you have a rubber tube full of water with a hole in it you only force the water out by increasing pressure on the outside of the tube, whereas if you can reduce the external pressure you can soon stop the flow of water. By reducing inter-thoracic and inter-abdominal pressure FMA could take the pressure off the lungs and so stop the haemorrhage. The proprietor of a famous old hotel in Brighton was cured in this way.

Bill then remarked that he had been thinking more of conscious direction applied to a specific trauma, say of the finger. FM replied by referring to the remarkable powers that some people have (all Russian women, he said, and also people like his own mother) to charm away warts. He told how his mother once removed a wart from his eyelid by touching the spot with a piece of raw meat which she afterwards buried in the ground.[7] The discussion then became general.

In the evening Jack Norris came to dinner and talked of his experiences in India during the war. He obviously understands little of the fundamentals of the work, such as 'ordering', for instance, speaking the whole time of 'treatment', but his views on the future development and training of teachers coincided with mine.

Tuesday 12th March

This afternoon FM raised three special points in the students' class. These were things that he said all students could, and should, watch when working among themselves. The first was the continuance of inhibition of the end when the time came to put the means-whereby into operation. He demonstrated that we all tend to desert the new means-whereby as soon as we feel a stimulus from the teacher that indicates that he is going to make some movement with us.

The second point was the stiffening of the legs and thighs at all times. He said it is easy to check whether you have stiffened the legs in getting into a chair and the thing to do was to continue getting in and out of the chair until the legs were free. It is useless to sit and try to free the legs simply by ordering under those circumstances.

The third point was the controlling of breathing whilst being worked upon. He pointed out that if you allow the head to go forward and up for the back to lengthen and widen to go back and allow the ribs to contract, that process did the breathing for you – that was breathing. Whereas if you continue to do what you call breathing while giving the above orders it defeats its own purpose and you will never gain control of your respiratory processes.

He said that students might help one another by placing their hands under each other's necks, with the forearms against the chest and back, so telling when the head was pulled back or down in making any movement. He emphasised the essential simplicity of the Technique and how we are all always seeking to complicate things. He instanced Burgess ('Mr B.' of *The UCL*) who had had a lesson today and suddenly said for the first time, 'You know, FM, we make too much fuss about this.' He also instanced James Harvey Robinson* who wrote 'The Philosopher's Stone', but was unteachable himself and died at 40.

Alma and Pat came to dinner. She told us about the situation in America. The essence is as follows. Dolly Daily* – who is training teachers of the Technique to undertake ordinary peda-gogy for the Quakers – has had less than three years training herself, is an ex-ballet dancer of some distinction with a very bad use of herself and little idea of the Technique. Trouble is mount-ing with the Quakers. Lulie Westfeldt* has been behaving rather strangely in a way that suggests some psychophysical imbalance: starving her maid, following people round the flat, petty meanness, wild accusations, and so on. Marjorie Barstow* is good, but nursing her father in the Middle West and so much out of the picture. D. Daily was a friend of Barstow. Both idolise AR.

Wednesday 13th March

FM told us how, this morning, he opened the door to a man who had come to see him without appointment and, contrary to his principle in these matters, he consented to see him. The man explained that he had been treated for years by psychoanalysists, psychologists and physiotherapists until he had 'no brain left'. He kept bursting into floods of tears. FM pointed out to him the shocking way in which he was using his body but, of course, it did not convey anything. There was great difficulty in getting rid of the poor chap.

FM next told of a case of a man who had come to him with a surgical boot with an iron on one foot[8] who removed it after the third lesson without FM's consent. The man never needed it again but FM was much apprehensive of the possible consequences when he first saw it and stated that this was not the sort of case he ever talked about because it did not constitute a 'real result'. Obviously it was something of a special sort that the man was doing to himself that he was able to stop when the proper stimulus was presented for him to do so.

Yesterday FM told how, as a young man, a doctor friend of his persuaded him to hoax a throat specialist for him. He went to the man simulating loss of voice. His throat was examined, diagnosis made and treatment prescribed. At the end of the interview FM thanked the specialist in his normal voice. The man was so angry that FM could not refrain from remarking, 'That showed what your diagnosis was worth!'

At the end of class FM asked whether we still remembered his three points of yesterday; the unstiffening of the knees, the non-controlling of breathing and the sticking to the means-whereby against the stimulus to make a movement. In the subsequent discussion it appeared that few had understood his remarks or remembered the sense of them.

I am very tired tonight, having experienced a bigger change to my co-ordination today than at any time for many years. Pat, Dorothy and I had a most interesting lunch together and later Dorothy took me out to tea. Discussing the future, we agreed that we must co-operate together and Dorothy mentioned that the teacher training activity in America was the greatest danger to our case against Jokl* in South Africa.[9]

Thursday 14th March

I asked FM today about Arbuthnot Lane.* He said that he was one of the doctors to whom he came with an introduction from Australia. He only saw him once when it was clear that Lane would not be of any help to him. He described him as a ruffian and added that when the full consequences were seen of his famous operations, for which he used to charge two hundred and fifty guineas, he had to retire from medicine. He made his money on the stock-exchange, being one of those people with no knowledge, but a natural flair for such matters.

I next asked FM to repeat again the point he had previously made about breathing. He then demonstrated and said that, if you ordered the neck to be free and the head forward and up to lengthen and widen the back, you automatically enlarged the thoracic cavity and so enabled atmospheric pressure to do its work. If you then went on with these orders to allow the ribs to contract, the air would be expelled. Thus you brought about an elastic, two-way reaction. His point was that that was breathing; if on the other hand, whilst giving these guiding orders, you continued to do what you considered breathing, you were in fact preventing the natural breathing process from taking place and trying to impose an artificial form of control on something that was already controlled naturally.

Someone then asked why it was necessary for him in working on a pupil to bring about the contraction of the ribs with the hand. He replied that it was a matter of giving the pupil the correct experience immediately, for to bring about the contraction by continuance with the orders alone would take a very long time. He pointed out that if you burnt your hand in the fire you did not forget the experience. Similarly once you have an experience the organism does not forget it. He said that people often fail to register such experiences because, instead of inhibiting and allowing the experience to be given to them, they try by means of physical effort to prevent themselves 'doing' and so increase tension as to make registration impossible. He went on to say that once the average person has had 20 or 30 lessons it is absolutely impossible for them to revert to exactly their old habits of misuse; and in some cases this effect is operative much sooner.

Also referring to breathing, he said that breathing brought about in the manner demonstrated and described above was brought about with a minimum of tension and also resulted in the minimum shock to the heart in changing from inspiration to expiration. Dr Drew confirmed this, saying that on the X-ray screen you can see the heart 'bumping'[10] as this change-over occurs in most people, but the bumping disappears when breathing is brought about by the proper means-whereby. FM referred to the case of Mr Rowntree*, who had a 'murmuring'[11] heart. The specialist who treated him whilst he was being worked upon declared that the different method of breathing caused the 'murmur' practically to disappear.

Later he mentioned a pupil who had come to him with an arm of which she had lost the use. She said this had come about when someone spilt a cup of hot tea down her back. He pointed out to us that this explanation could not be the cause of the trouble. The cause must have been in what she did with herself by way of reaction to this scalding. He proposed to take her, although he did not like the feel of the joint in her arm. He intended to work on her first and get her general co-ordination straightened out and, after that, he would have the joint X-rayed, if necessary, to see if anything could be done with it.

The other day, with regard to the Burgess case, he told us that a certain orthopaedic specialist had told B. that what had been done in his case was a miracle. B. replied that FMA would disagree that there was any miraculous element in it but that it was the demonstrable and logical result of his principle. The interesting fact was that this specialist had at least a dozen similar cases to B.'s on his hands but he never sent a single patient to FM.

Alma Frank described a large pupil who had caused her much trouble. FM characterised him as an 'hulking microbe'.

Tuesday 19th March

On Friday I went down to Somerset to stay with Dr Francis for the weekend. The students' class was in the morning but produced nothing noteworthy. I returned on Monday morning in time for a little work before lunch. The afternoon class again produced nothing noteworthy but at lunch-time I heard that Irene Tasker* has been doing no teaching in London out of regard for FM and yet finds difficulty in getting to see him even, and is told nothing about the S. Africa case!

Wednesday 20th March

On Tuesday Dilys and I had dinner at Veglio's and then went to see *A Woman Disappeared* and today we went out with Jack Norris to see *Follow the Girls* at His Majesty's and on to a dinner-dance at Ciro's. My use is improving steadily in spite of all this gaiety.

There has been nothing especially memorable about the students' class, except the following. FM said that he was a fool not to spend at least an hour a day working on himself in the same way that he used to do and that we do now. Pat and Dorothy told me that FM pulled himself down very badly during a recent bout of 'flu. He said to a pupil the other day, 'You know you will go away from here and say that I have been giving you a lesson and it won't be true. You have been giving me a lesson and I don't want one!'

Thursday 21st March

Dorothy, Pat and I had lunch together as usual. In class FM talked and demonstrated brilliantly, but there was nothing very new in it. He did mention that Waterston* had assured him with his own lips that there was no mechanism known to physiology that could move the head forward and up. This bore out his own contention that the 'forward and up' direction was a matter of non-interference but of allowing something to take place naturally. Similarly, the muscles across the back, the anti-gravity muscles, never tire, therefore FM argued that they must be particularly insensitive, which was why he used a book against the back of a chair to come back to.

Regarding science, scientific method and the procedure of this work, he agreed the following statement. Scientists carry out a large number of experiments to establish certain specific facts and at the end of the process they vaguely perceive some general principle involved. We take a principle and apply it. This supplies its own operational verification in process but also leads to the establishment of certain specific facts in course of the process.

After the class I had to do some typing concerning the South African case. Later Dilys, Dorothy, Pat and I went out to see *A Man about the House* with Flora Robson and had food afterwards at the Gate Restaurant. They all came back here for a cup of tea.

FM wants to see all the old students together on Saturday, so my trip to Bournemouth is postponed until Saturday afternoon.

Friday 22nd March

Dilys had lunch with the rest of us and then in the evening she and I went to see *Caesar and Cleopatra*, after which we had a very good dinner of turkey at the Duck Inn in Marylebone High Street.

In class this morning I asked FM about the evolution of the 'book'.[12] He replied as follows. He wanted something to place behind his back in the chair in order to feel that part of his back. At first he tried an ordinary book. That was too heavy and tended to fall out of place. Then he tried tying it to the back of the chair with tape. That was not satisfactory because it was inclined to stimulate him to pull down and shorten his back. Next he tried an empty cigar box, but that slipped too easily. Finally he hit on the idea of a velvet-covered cigar box. This would stay in position by tending to cling to his clothes, but at the same time it would slide easily on the polished back of the chair and so enable him to lengthen up from it without difficulty.

The purpose of the cigar box was (*a*) to stimulate the somewhat insensitive region of the anti-gravity muscles and (*b*) to stimulate the shoulder-blades to slip into place. He said that he does not often use the 'book' himself now, because he can get what he wants with other means by his hands, but he advises us to do so in working with pupils and on ourselves. In the latter case, however, he remarked that there is some danger of losing our length in putting the 'book' in place.

In answer to an enquiry of Alma's, he said that he varied the form of the instruction 'to put the knees away' or 'to let the knees fall apart' and so on, just as he could get the pupil to respond. In any case it was an order and the 'doing', so to say, took place by itself when consent was given to put the whole means-whereby into operation.

He made some remarks about his use of the term 'inhibition'. It had caused anxiety among many of his friends due to the extreme prejudice against it. Dewey* undertook a long railway journey specially to warn him about it. What everybody had overlooked was that inhibition is a form of volition.

With regard to Waterston, FM saw him once only but had a long and friendly interview lasting for about two hours and including a demonstration. Waterston wanted to carry out certain physiological experiments, or tests, but when he realised that the basic factor in the whole Technique was volitional, i.e. that the primary thing was the so-called mental, and that all the physiological side, including the sub-occipital muscles, was purely secondary, he saw that it was outside his province. FM first made the point about the absence of mechanism to take the head forward and up and Waterston confirmed it.

Saturday 23rd March

This morning FM held a special class for the graduate teachers from 11 to 12 o'clock, as follows. Marjory and Bill, Dick and Elisabeth [Walker*], Alma and Dorothy (although not a graduate), Pat and myself. Irene Stewart watched, Margaret Goldie did not appear.

FM pointed out that we should always work on a pupil with the knees going forward and away, and never with straight legs. In order to achieve this position care must be taken to keep length and allow the head to go forward and up as a primary, and not to throw the hips forward as a primary.

To the hands of another person placed on the hips or back there should be no change in weight, whether the teacher is in erect posture or allowing the knees to go forward and away.

When the teacher puts his hands on the pupil he must do so with free wrists so that whatever change may be made in attitude or posture the touch of the hands will remain unchanged.

When taking the head the work must, first of all, be done purely by the fingers; that is to say, there should be no increase of muscular activity in the arms until the pupil is actually to be moved. The forearm of the hand which takes the back of the head should lie along the pupil's back. Hands should only be placed on the pupil briefly to commence with, for, if the wrong stimulus is given at first, the misdirection will persist for a long time, just as the heart of a decerebrate animal will continue to beat after the cerebrum has been removed. A fresh start must be made in such a case to render the inhibition effective.

To promote lengthening and widening of the back and to stimulate the anti-gravity muscles to do this work, one hand may be placed across the scapulae, the other on the clavicles. Then, gently ease the scapulae into place and encourage the chest to drop by a gentle pressure on the clavicles. If the knees are now encouraged to move forward and away from each other, the pupil will be automatically brought out of the chair.

I found using my hands on this occasion very difficult and frightening because I lacked all sense of confidence in them. However, I see clearly that practice is the thing, for both tiredness and ineptitude are only the result of one's failure to employ the proper means-whereby.

Monday 25th March
Yesterday I spent at Bournemouth with my aunt and uncle from where I returned today. Poor Dilys was to have lunched

with me but instead had to rush to Birmingham on a false alarm about the children, from which she returned in the evening.

Meanwhile I had arranged for Irene Tasker to have dinner with us so took her to the Waldorf instead. We had a long and interesting talk lasting three hours and covering most aspects of the future. She cannot come into any scheme during FM's lifetime but will run a small school for children in Hampshire once she gets the S. African affair settled. The S. A. affair looks black. Pirow,* the S. African quisling, has been briefed for the defence and much mud will be slung.

I am to take over much of the secretarial work at Ashley Place.

Tuesday 26th March

I had lunch with Alma today at Overtons. The picture of the future of the work grows more and more clear. Alma approves my old proposals for the working of an Institute. Eric de Peyer* was in this afternoon, much pulled down. I had tea with Dorothy. Her husband returned yesterday after his plane, a York, had belly-landed in Tripoli. The children came back safely today. I am very tired.

Wednesday 27th March

This was a much better day from the point of view of my use. I had tea with Alma and she repeated a story of FM's: how he used to follow pupils out of his room, working on them to the last, just on the point of getting something: 'But now', says he, 'I can give it to them whether they want it or not.' The class was unmemorable.

In the evening Dilys and I had dinner with her mother and father. We were to have had it at Whitehall Court but the ladies arrived too late, so had an excellent meal at Veglio's instead.

Thursday 28th March

Today I did a really hard day's work, starting by giving Mother a good turn on the couch in the morning and ending by giving Dilys one in the evening. During the day I worked on Pat and Alma, also with satisfactory results, and typed and revised a long letter for FM.

The class did not produce anything very special except some observations on end-gaining. FM observed that the human race must be made not to concentrate on ends in the way everybody does.

Friday 29th March

In class this morning FM again referred to Waterston. The interview was arranged by Murdoch* and Waterston's intention was to write a book on 'the human being in action', or some such title. At the end of it FM said, 'Of course you can do all that you intend to do and you still won't have even considered the important things about the subject you are dealing with.' Waterston was much surprised until FM pointed out that thinking, willing or wishing, inhibition, the nature of feeling-tones, habit and so on all lay outside the scope of his physiology. Then he agreed.

This led on to the whole question of conception. Irving* used to keep FM very often for a couple of hours after a lesson just to talk about these things. He would say, 'Once I used to send my young people to watch the great artists, but I have given that up now for they only copy their mistakes'. To Shaw, FM made the same point that once you ask a person with a defective manner of use to carry out any conception, you are placing them in a danger zone. Price,* the great golfer, saw this in connection with trying all his life to keep his right shoulder down, which caused his chest trouble. FM also spoke again on one of his favourite texts, that if in research you know what you are looking for you will never find anything new.

In the evening, I had dinner with him and AR at the Café Royal. We had a lot of interesting talk about different aspects of the future of the work. He thinks that the S. African business is fairly safe now, even if it comes to trial. Of Eric de Peyer, he says that he has seen something at last and will be useful to us. He has some hopes for Charles [Neil*] too. With regard to Erika and Duncan [Whittaker*] he thinks that the latter will do a big thing for us one day when he has reached the head of his profession. At present he has to think of his superiors all the time and has already done a courageous thing in rejecting their advice about Erika's TB in face of his own.

He told us about E.V. Lucas,* when chairman of the board of Methuen, saying that he could sell huge numbers of *Constructive Conscious Control of the Individual* if it were rewritten in intelligible language. FM promptly offered him a thousand pounds to do this, provided he put down what FM wished to say. When this offer was rejected he increased it to two thousand. E.V. strenuously objected to the title of *The Use of the Self* because he said it would be connected in people's minds with 'the abuse of the self'. According to FM, this was characteristic.

With regard to S. Africa, he said how gratified he was that one of his teachers should have been able to go out there and build up such a wonderfully loyal band of supporters. They had offered to raise the £5,000 for the trial among themselves, if he would let them.

Miss Webb* once spoke of the remarkable effect of good food on FM. As a young man in Australia a friend who had seen him before lunch might observe on meeting him afterwards, 'Hello Alexander, you look a different man from when I saw you a while ago', and the answer was, 'Oh, I have just had a good meal.'

Monday 1st April

On Saturday morning FM rang up to say that he had just had a letter from the Ministry of Labour & National Service asking for a prospectus of the training course so as to be able to answer enquiries from ex-servicemen desirous of taking up the work as a career. Some official recognition at last.[13]

On Sunday lunched with E.S.P. Haynes.

Today I typed some more copies of the letter to the Cabinet Ministers. Ellen Wilkinson's secretary rang up for details about the young man concerned. This was a very quick and satisfactory response to the first of the copies sent off on Friday. I had lunch with Dick and Elisabeth and discussed schools for the children.

This evening I had a drink with Pat and Alma. She was distressed because FM has been getting after her for pulling herself down to teach. He said she was pulling herself down worse than anybody on Saturday morning. I think he is probably quite right and shall not be convinced that he is attacking Alma for other reasons unless evidence is forthcoming but, given her emotional background, it is hard for her to bear and I don't know whether it is really the wisest approach.

Tuesday 2nd April

In class today FM pointed out that I am still holding on badly under the chin. He advised much work in front of the mirrors to overcome this. Dilys went out to the theatre so I was home early to look after the children.

Wednesday 3rd April

I worked nearly all day on the prospectus for the Ministry of Labour. In the evening I had drinks and food with Pat and Charles Neil. The latter told us much of his experiences in India. With regard to the future of the work he seems co-operative but will obviously go his own way to a large extent.

Sunday 7th April

On Thursday the 4th, Dick and Elisabeth came to dinner and I completed the prospectus. On Friday 5th, I visited E.S.P.H. at Lincoln's Inn. In the evening Pat and I went out to Crystal Palace to have dinner with Dorothy and husband. Yesterday we took the children to Pat's for lessons in the morning. Today we took them to Hampstead Heath in the afternoon.

These days I am growing lazy, which is why this diary is suffering, but little of great moment has happened to record. Only in class on Thursday FM was good on end-gaining and means-whereby. He said that when you get up in the morning you know that you are coming to town but you don't allow this knowledge to hinder you from carrying out the normal routine of getting dressed, having breakfast and so. So with getting into or out of a chair.

Monday 8th April

I had a haircut at Peter Robinson's early in the morning. Afterwards I did some work on Patrick and then gave John Gosse a lesson. This was the first lesson I have given since I returned. Lunch was, as usual, with Pat and Dorothy.

In the class I asked about J. [Gosse]. FM said that it was very doubtful if he would ever learn to inhibit and, until he did so, it was hopeless to expect any improvement. I told him that J. had proposed giving up speaking for a fortnight and doing intensive work on himself meanwhile. He said that might help, only it was doubtful whether, even then, J. would be prepared to do the necessary work. He said J. is a nice boy. 'I like him very much or I should have kicked him out long ago. You can lead a horse to water . . .', etc.

He repeated the story about the American woman who made a special journey across for lessons and paid four guineas a day for three months. After the second or third lesson he said, 'You are not inhibiting', and she got very angry, saying, 'How can you know what is going on inside my brain?' A long time afterwards she wrote from America saying she was sorry and FM was quite right, she was not inhibiting and had no intention of doing so. FM said they all think they know better how to get it their way.

In the evening I gave mother a lesson at five. Then I met Dilys and Jack Norris and we went off to dinner at a Jewish restaurant in Soho, and then on to the Odeon to see a film about prisoners of war entitled *The Captive Heart*.

Tuesday 9th April

I spent the greater part of today in writing a letter for FM to Ellen Wilkinson. In the evening I went with mother to see a farce at the Globe Theatre entitled *Whilst the Sun Shines*.

Wednesday 10th April

I finished E.W.'s letter and in the evening went with Dilys to Pat's house to help move furniture. At tea time I had a long talk with Dick and Elisabeth about nursery schools for the children, and the possibility of dividing the class into two parts.

FM talked a lot in class today. Of taking pupils he said that, if you always ensured that they kept their length and did not pull down to do anything but always stopped them as soon as they showed any signs of doing so, you could not go wrong. He attributed Irene's success in South Africa to the fact that she always took her pupils for about 4 months and would never let them get away with anything.

Thursday 11th April to Wednesday 17th April
Term finished on Wednesday the 17th. The diary was much neglected throughout the last few days owing to so many social activities in the evenings. In brief, the course of events was as follows.

On Thursday 11th, Dilys and I went to the cinema in the evening. On Friday 12th, John Gosse came to dinner and we had a good deal of talk about the work. On Saturday 13th, we all visited Dick and Elisabeth at Hampstead for tea. On Sunday I walked and lunched with E.S.P.H. On Monday 15th we were to have had an Oyster Party, but the oysters failed to materialize, so Dorothy and David, Pat, Dilys and I spent the evening at The Doves instead. On Tuesday 16th, the oysters did come and so Dick and Elisabeth, Tom, Pat and myself foregathered to eat them. On Wednesday 17th, Dorothy, David, Pat and I ate oysters for lunch and in the evening I had dinner at the Café Royal with FM, Margaret Goldie and Irene Stewart.

À propos of this it should be mentioned that we have now secured a flat in Carlyle Place, subject only to the approval of the Westminster Council, so we can now think in longer terms, particularly of a full-time secretary.[14]

Alma returns to America on Saturday 20th. She parted with FM on most amiable terms. He told her that he is much disturbed by reports from America and disclaims all responsibility for activities there. He did not sign certificates for the training course over there. Alma thinks that before she could recommend people to come over here for the course the class would have to be smaller and more individual work be given by FM.

G.B. Shaw badly wanted to see FM and he went to see him on Thursday 18th.

Working on Pat on Thursday evening I found the great importance of using the hands as opposed to the fingers.

Monday 6th May

I returned to work at Ashley Place this morning after visiting the tailor to order a new suit. There was no news and the day passed quietly, but in the evening I was very tired indeed.

Tuesday 7th May

This morning I took Mr F. C. C. Watts* out to lunch at the Waldorf. We discussed the future and he was twice good enough to express his hopes and confidence in me. He asked what was to happen to the copyright of the books on FM's death and asked how we could ensure that his executors would permit the use of his name in connection with any institute. He also told me how he first came to have lessons after the last war, at the age of 29. All he had in the world was £50 in Post Office savings and FM's fee was then 4 guineas a lesson. He agreed to pay three instalments of £25 each and drew all of his money out of the Post Office.

In the afternoon we had an interesting class in which FM remarked that he had had a pupil that morning who never put a foot wrong in a first lesson. He said that one could always tell whether a pupil was ordering by the speed of reaction, for instance in getting into or out of a chair. I talked with FM later and I am to see him next week to discuss my own future and the future of the association. Later I had a talk with Pat and we argued the main principles to be observed in the conduct of any such association. At night I was again too tired to do any further work.

Wednesday 8th May

In the morning I worked hard on the students but missed much of the afternoon class owing to typing that had to be done.

After class I gave Alfred Smart a lesson. In the evening I met Hugh Greenwood at the Bag o' Nails and had dinner with him at Veglio's.

Thursday 9th May

I worked with the students again in the morning and then took Irene Stewart out to lunch to talk about the future. She asked me when I was going to resume teaching again and said that FM had told her that I was in a bad mess and he wanted me to take things easy for a time. We argued about future plans but I can see that the situation will be very complex and need tactful handling. Marjory's and Bill's attitude now seem very important.

In the class FM spoke of the reactions of people in the mass and how we are lost when we lose sight of the individual. That set me thinking. Afterwards I gave Smart another lesson and returned home early, very tired.

FM told two stories of some interest today. During the time that he was in America the Christian Science[15] people sent him a pupil, a daughter of a very fine healthy family who was a 'throwback'. The Technique did something for her but not much. However, as a result of this, the head of the Christian Science Movement visited him. She told him that she personally had been cured by Christian Science but expressed the wish to have lessons. It was obvious as she spoke that she had the symptoms of at least four recognisable pathological conditions but FM ignored this, merely saying, 'If you have been cured by Christian Science why do you want to come to me for lessons?' However, she came but, at about the fourth lesson, FM found it necessary to do something to try and bring her 'into communication with her reason'. He said, 'You know, you are a terrible woman – such a liar and so deliberate with it also.' Of course she was very upset, so he reminded her of how she had told him of being cured by Christian Science when it was obvious that she was a very sick woman. She admitted it and after that her lessons went better and she made considerable improvement. Someone in the class asked, 'And did she give up her Christian Science?' 'No', replied FM, 'I'm afraid she had too good a job to do that.'

FM also told us that he was in a very friendly correspondence with Woodrow Wilson* before the last war, although the war intervened to prevent their meeting. Wilson used to say to his students, 'Remember that concentration is death'.

Friday 10th May

Dorothy Drew has been having great pain in her back. Her husband said, 'I think perhaps you should see a doctor', and, 'Of course, if you will indulge in these amateur athletics ...' I worked hard with the students until class. Then I had lunch with Pat. In the afternoon more work with students and gave a lesson to Alfred Smart, who tells me he has been having heart trouble. In the evening, a drink with Pat and dinner with Mrs Gaze.

Monday 13th May

Douglass Price-Williams* received calling-up papers this morning so I had to devote my time to composing a last desperate appeal to the Ministry of Labour for him. Then Mrs Drew – Dorothy's mother – fell on the front steps and injured her leg. It proved afterwards that the femur was broken so we had great difficulty in getting her out to the car. FM got Pat and me to take her weight, while he took her head and Irene S. moved her knees. He bullied her unmercifully for pulling down. Then he took her weight himself whilst I supported his arm – he almost exhausted himself. The poor woman continued to pull herself down, which was not surprising when the bone was broken. Eventually Pat got a chair and we carried her out. How astonishing that this situation was not hit upon before! I should have thought that they might have verified that the bone was broken to begin with.

There was only time for a sandwich for lunch and I had much typing to do in the class time. However, I got my turns in from FM. Then I had to give Smart a lesson. What an agony this is to me when I am not in very best condition. I pull down and know that I am giving nothing or very little with my hands so I endeavour to do less, lest I should pull my pupil down. Then I don't seem to be achieving anything in the lesson so I watch the clock anxiously and long for the time to pass. However, FM came in and saw Smart today and thought he was going ahead pretty well.

Afterwards we had tea and Jean MacInnes turned up. After that I went to Paddington and met Dilys, the children and their luggage, and saw them home. How lovely it is to have them back once more.

I forgot to record the other day that FM said that A. J. Balfour* was always being held up to him as an example of an absolutely brilliant man, successful in all spheres, with a shocking use of himself. But he was a relative of Lytton and Lytton once said, 'What nonsense – I have known him for over thirty years and he has never enjoyed a day free from some illness in his life.'

Tuesday 14th May

I went straight to Peter Robinson's first of all for a haircut. Afterwards I worked with the students. Douglass has been re-prieved – I suppose due to yesterday's efforts. Lunch with Pat and the Drew family at the old place. FM remarked in class that he used to get annoyed with people who did not see what he saw. Now he realised that no-one could be expected to do so unless they had had similar experience. He said that the best policy was to go on and on repeating things to people without taking much notice of what they said and one day they would come to understand. Smart was much better this afternoon – or was it me? – anyway I took him on the table, which is always better. After tea I hurried home. What a joy it is to have the children and, above all, Dilys to come home to.

Wednesday 15th May

This morning I had to meet Aunty Alice at Waterloo and then take her to Dickens and Jones where we all had lunch to-gether – the whole family of us. After lunch I went to Nº 16 for the students' class, about which I can recall nothing memorable. Then there was Smart to be taken again; after which, tea and straight home to spend a quiet evening with the family.

Thursday 16th May

This was rather an important and memorable day. In the morning I gave John Gosse a lesson and, to my great satisfaction, he observed: 'I know what is the trouble with me, I don't really want to do this.' So, at last, he is seeing the light.

I had lunch by myself and returned early. FM came into the students' class rather early and invited me to have dinner with him and our talk tonight. He spoke of education and teaching people to believe instead of showing them what not to believe, and also the harmful effects of stifling criticism of anything.

This lead to the rather favourite topic of Roman Catholicism. He said that a man must be a great scoundrel to allow himself to be elected Pope, and he spoke of the process of Papal election as being as bad, if not worse, than the process of presidential election in the USA. No doubt but he is right in the fundamental sense for, if the whole process whereby belief is established and encouraged is wrong and opposed to the process whereby belief ought to be established, it is a terrible thing to take responsibility for leading people astray and, in effect, teaching what you know to be untrue.

Referring to his own schooling, FM said that they could never make anything of him at school. He used to argue with the masters and dispute every statement that was held up for his belief. If they then referred him to a book he would ask how the writer of the book knew it to be true. They used to send him up for thrashings but he still came back for more. He would fight anybody and had a terrible temper. Only his mother really understood him. His father would say, 'How can you do a thing if you don't mean to do it?' And he had no answer to make. Now, of course, he would say, 'Because of my stupid quick reaction which causes me to act before I think.'

He first started thinking along the lines of the work from the age of about 16. In the end, the headmaster of his school used to have him round to his house and work with him in the evenings and that was the only real schooling he ever got. On Saturdays he would take him out duck-shooting to quieten him down. They used to leave him alone at school during the day to go his own way. He used to pass all examinations and win all prizes with the greatest of ease and later they used to try and discourage him from working too hard.

Returning to the other matter, he recently had a pupil, a RC in a very high position in this country, who asked, 'Will your work interfere with my Faith?' FM replied that he could not set a very high valuation on his faith to ask such a question. After class I took Smart for a lesson at 4.30. Afterwards FM, Margaret Goldie and I went to the Café Royal where we had a good dinner, a good bottle of French white wine and some good talk. FM remarked that he never had understood how it was possible to believe anything without first experiencing it. His own father, he said, was a man of very unusual and wide views in most things but he believed (FM thought) quite literally in Heaven and Hell and that anyone not of the Church of England faith was utterly lost.

Talking on quite a different topic, he mentioned that his brother, A. R. Alexander, served as a trooper with an Australian Unit in the Boer War and was one of only four survivors when all the rest were wiped out in an ambush.

After this, we returned to N⁰ 16, where Margaret left us and we settled down for a chat. He asked me, 'What are your troubles?' I said that I didn't think I had any. And he said that he didn't think that I had either. He then said he would pay me £5 per week and half the fees for whatever teaching I did, guaranteeing me a minimum of £10 a week. This being the same arrangement that he has with Pat and, I think, very generous. This is to commence from June the first.

With regard to the future of the work he proposed that, as soon as Bill comes back, we should discuss ways and means of forming a partnership to include all the present teachers, Dorothy Drew, Tom Davidson and Guy [Baron], Dick and Elisabeth. These would then inherit the work and employ others on a similar basis to that on which we are now employed. He said that, apart from this, the future was safeguarded to a reasonable extent with his executors, but I did not press for details here.

We next discussed a number of topics briefly as follows. The desirability of his doing much more writing now and producing a journal in the future, the latter he thinks being a better means of stimulating thinking than more large volumes. À propos of this he is in favour of a full-time secretary to help him and do our office work. He wants the school well established soon because he regards that as being our most important responsibility. He is most unhappy about the American affair and even Marjorie Barstow has gone clean off the rails. She has been writing to him claiming to have made wonderful new discoveries. However, he will have nothing to do with them.

With regard to the case, it cannot now come to trial before next March. This, at least, will mean that his South African counsel will be able to conduct his part in the commission over here. I spoke about the omissions from *MSI* of the Dewey and Kallen letters: he thinks this might be rectified in a pamphlet.[16]

After all this we went down to the kitchen and made some wonderful china tea and had some light chat, telling tales and so on. FM loves a good Rabelaisian tale, but is a little spinsterish about them none the less.

Reverting to the serious talk that we were having before, he said he thought he ought to go out and about more. As a young man he once travelled to Hobart intending to start teaching there. On the train he met the editor of the Hobart *Mercury* who became interested in him after some talk and introduced him to Tennison, the manager of the bank there. Shortly afterwards he was introduced to one of the big clubs there and quickly made many friends. Later still, meeting the editor in the street, the latter said 'Many people have invited you to go to their houses and you have refused. These people would do anything for you. You ought to go about and see more of them.'

After all of this talk I left him at 11.15 and returned home.

Friday 17th May
This morning I went in as usual and took Smart at 11 o'clock. At 11.30 there was the students' class. The man I wrote to on Tuesday about Douglass telephoned FM yesterday and promised to do the best he could. After class I had lunch with Dad at Veglio's and did not get back until 3 o'clock. After tea I took Mr Lee for

Pat and then returned home. There is nothing more frustrating than working on a pupil, getting no result and knowing that you are pulling yourself down more and more. I think that the only way out is to arrange to do half an hour's work with Pat each day.

Monday 20th May

Irene Stewart has been down with a cold over the weekend so I have had to do part of her teaching.

In the afternoon FM referred to the evolution of hands on the back of a chair, saying that it was put into the book (*CCC*) in response to the request of those who wanted to know how much tension should be used in the arms for any given purpose.

With regard to the whispered *ah*, this was evolved when a singing teacher called Mr Lawrence pointed out that the perfect *ah* required the removal of the upper lip from the teeth. This naturally resulted in an ugly grimace. FM then got the idea of a natural smile to achieve the same result.

An excellent house was offered to FM today, № 11, Chester Square.

This evening Hugh Greenwood came to dinner and we chatted of not much all night.

Tuesday 21st May

Today I had to start at 9 o'clock to take one of Irene's pupils and so worked hard all day. In the evening Pat and Margaret and I went out together, taking FM with us. We went to the Path-finder Association and had drinks and then on to Veglio's for a meal. Here Dilys joined us and an excellent meal it was. FM said it had really done him good. He gave us a bottle and a half of burgundy to drink with the meal. We had lovely chat and excellent talk, but I was so tired that I fear it is lost.

Wednesday 22nd May

Once more I took Irene's pupils for her and I was very tired when the end of the day came. However, my teaching is improving and I don't think I am pulling down quite so badly. Pat came to supper in the evening. Afterwards we went out for a drink, but the beer at the Raven was so vile that we could not drink much of it and so returned soon to bed.

Thursday 23rd May

Today I took Irene's pupils again – seven in all – starting at 9 o'clock in the morning. John Gosse was very difficult but has improved none the less. Smart was going well today. I'm tired but not nearly so tired as yesterday. I think that FM has taken the house, 11 Chester Square; the experts' reports on it are very favourable. Marjory and Bill came back from Switzerland yesterday.

Friday 24th May

This morning Irene was back again so I had an easier day, taking only my own pupils. Mr Turner has caused me some misgivings and I wonder if he is going as well as I had supposed. A cable came from S. Africa today to say that the costs to be paid into Court are £1,000 by the end of July and £1,000 three weeks prior to the trial of the case. I think, very satisfactory.

Smart was going well today and wants to come in for lessons for another week. I got FM to look at him to see how he is going and he was very pleased. This is naturally a great satisfaction and encouragement to me.

Difficulties have arisen about the house, but we still have the flat to fall back upon.

In the evening I met Hugh Greenwood at the Bag of Nails for a drink and we then went on to Vyeni's in Charlotte Street where Dilys joined us for dinner. It was a rotten meal – I thought – but we went on to the Pathfinder Club afterwards.

Monday 27th May

This morning started with the arrival of a most interesting letter from Mr Morgan, a relative of Miss Edith Thomas* in Szeged. She is alive and fairly well, but I now hope to be able to contact her personally.

At Ashley Place I took Crundall, the optician, first of all. He was very difficult. Irene tells me that he has had osteopathic treatment – that would account for it. Next there was Turner. I took him lying-down and he seemed to be going well again.

I went out with Dorothy Drew to lunch at the Green Man at Great Portland Street: she intends to devote her time to teaching when she has finished, she says.

FM in class spoke of the general debasing of standards and remarked that people who were responsible for taking the lowest standard as the standard for all, as in Trades Unionism, should be put in prison.

After tea I took Smart who still seems to be going well. His doctor has put him on to consult a specialist about his heart, but one cannot see what good that will do.

I think that my own use and my teaching is improving a great deal but I am tired by the end of the day.

Tuesday 28th May

This morning I went into Ashley Place fairly early to attend to the correspondence. I had five pupils to take which kept me fairly busy. One was John Vicary* whom I take and for whom I also feel sorry. His use is shocking and I don't think he has any desire to do anything about it. Considering that he has had so much work, and been to the school in the bargain, that is bad; but perhaps only what one might expect.

I had lunch with Pat and Dorothy and we talked of one Mary Lord for secretary. She seems to have everything we want but would probably not be content with that but want to teach anyway. In the evening I had dinner at Veglio's with FM and AR, Marjory and Bill and Irene Stewart. Half way through the meal who should walk in but my father.

We had a lot of good talk. FM told about AR having the middle finger of his left hand amputated without an anaesthetic. As a young man in Auzzie he shot the top off accidentally with a gun. He made the surgeon take it off right at the knuckle without an anaesthetic and it healed in a way that the doctors had never seen before. The supposed reason was that AR had been wanting to ride in an amateur steeplechase and was overweight. Consequently he had been taking Epsom Salts for some time past to get his weight down. This had apparently improved the healing quality of his flesh.

FM said that so many pupils say to one, 'Oh, but Nature will prevent us from going wrong'. This belief in Nature is astonishingly inconsistent like so many human beliefs for, if it is then pointed out to them that Nature will cause the head to go forward and up if allowed to do so, these same people do not believe it.

The Chester Square house is on again, the owners having reverted to the original price. He wrote to them and pointed out that if they increased the price on him like that they would have to pay his surveyors' fees. It was just a 'try on' on their part – an old dirty trick.

Wednesday 29th May

Once again I went in early to deal with the correspondence. Then I had Crundall whom I find very trying and difficult. He suffers from digestive troubles which form a vicious circle with his manner of use. I worked with the students and lunched with Pat.

In class FM referred to G. S. Lee.* He read the books, then stole the idea, so far as he could, and published a book of his own. Then he came for lessons and ran up an account of $5,000 of which he never paid a penny. Next, he tried to teach the work for himself and finally he sent his daughter over to England to try and get lessons from FM (she didn't).

Turner rang up this morning wanting to interrupt his lessons to take an engagement in Germany. I spoke to him on the phone. FM advised never discuss such matters with people over the telephone, always make them come and see you. Smart came. He is going well and is keen to come into the work. His heart specialist could find nothing organically wrong and advised nothing. Haynes rang up to say that he won his fight over his Chambers. The other side climbed down at the door of the Court. Watts sent me this morning two unbound copies of *The Universal Constant*.

Turner came for his lesson and remarked that a girl in his recent show had had lessons when she was eighteen and thinking of being a school-teacher. Now she earns her living displaying her shape, which I gather is a nice shape at that. Turner finds that his improving use make it less easy to play the clarionette.

Mr Scott came to me for a lesson. He has had about thirty. He remarked that I seemed to pull more on the head than the others – ruinous words – I must have been getting tired and pulling down. Dr Pilcher* came for his lesson and I worked hard on him – too hard for I was exhausted by 6.15. So I had a sandwich and a glass of beer before going home.

As a postscript to the 28th, I should add that FM spoke of his visit to GBS, who is now very old and weak but quite happy. One of the main themes of their conversation was that it is a great pity that a man should have to die at a time of life when he has acquired so much valuable experience. When Shaw was coming for lessons FM once asked him, 'Now do something for me, go home and eat a good plate of fat beef and drink a glass of burgundy with it.' GBS looked very serious and said, 'I must think about that.' When Mrs Shaw heard about it she was amazed to hear that he had not refused immediately. When he next came in for his lesson, two or three days later, he said, 'You know, Alexander, I would do a great deal for you, but I cannot do that.' FM replied, 'Very well, but please always remember what I asked you.' Two years later the old man was down with pernicious anaemia and now he has to keep alive on liver-extract and so on.[17]

Thursday 30th May

I went in fairly early again to write letters and then worked with the students. Before lunch I took Pilcher but continue to find him heavy and difficult. In the class I worked on the students a little for the first time but I find I still use myself very badly to teach. After class there was Smart, who was rather heavyish, and then, after tea, Andrews. I wish my teaching were better.

I have a notion to write a little explanatory pamphlet about the work now and print it over the holiday. An objection to the work has occurred to me today. Granted that manner of use is so important and far-reaching in its influence, how do we know that we can change and improve the manner of use to any extent that is really worthwhile? Look at Smart developing heart trouble after all these years of work, look at my mother, look at Crundall and hosts of others. Can we be sure that the degree of solid benefit derived from lessons is at all proportionate to the imagined benefits of grateful pupils? In other words, how much is it worth it?

Friday 31st May

Turner was going well this morning. In the class FM spoke of Dawson of Penn* [who was] always hostile to him. Once he was returning in a car from some function including Dawson and Meyers, the head of the Institute of Industrial Psychology. Meyers said to Dawson, 'Why are you so hostile to Alexander? What in your training and experience can justify it? You have learnt anatomy and physiology and yet if I were to examine you in either subject you would remember nothing about it. You know very little about my subject but you know nothing at all about Alexander's.'

On another famous occasion after a great deal of talk Dawson said, 'I think I begin to see the light.' Alexander retorted, 'Do you, Lord Dawson? Thank God!' The company, of course, roared.

Smart was going poorly in the afternoon. After tea I had Pilcher and took him lying down. It was quite an interesting lesson.

Monday 3rd June

FM had a long letter from Berrangé* this morning, giving a very cheerful and optimistic valuation of the judgement regarding the security and the future of the case.

Crundall had a lesson on the couch and went pretty well. He had osteopathic treatment last four years ago and doesn't believe in its lasting value. I watched Pilcher's lesson with great pleasure; FM made the two points about belief in Nature and the nature of the head to go forward and up, and also about the absurdity of wondering whether you would go wrong when carrying out a reasoned procedure. Later, I took Andrews and had him going fairly well. Afterwards, I went with Dilys to Ealing to visit Alan Dunning. Turner, by the way, had an excellent lesson before going to India.

Tuesday 4th June

This was quite a normal sort of day with no excitement until evening when we went to the Savoy to meet W/Cdr Russell and wife, Frank Campbell and wife, Peter Landon and wife, Alan and Ivy, Trevor and Paddy and a spare girl. A lovely party which ended in a nightclub on Stretton Street at 3.30 in the morning.

Wednesday 5th June

What a hangover! But I probably did some of my best work today on account of having to watch my own conditions so carefully. FM and many others went to the Derby so we had to stay behind to hold the fort. Trevor stayed with us for the night.

Thursday 6th June

I worked nearly all day on another letter to Ellen Wilkinson. I had only one pupil, Pilcher, and he was going very nicely. The only special lesson learned was that FM remarked that in writing about the work you should never put down anything that you can't demonstrate. The Bishop of Kensington came to dinner for a Confirmation so at home there was a bit of a flap.

Friday 7th June

This morning the students' class was very early and afterwards I had but one pupil. We finished at midday for a week's holiday and I spent the afternoon writing letters and clearing up.

My co-ordination has now vastly improved and so has my teaching, I am doing less and less with my hands to bring about better results, all of which is most encouraging. During this holiday I hope to get many things done, notably a paper to be entitled *An Introduction to the Work of F. Matthias Alexander* which can be issued in pamphlet form 'for the guidance of all concerned'. In the evening Dilys and I went to see a poor thing at the cinema called *Caravan*.

Monday 17th June

We returned to work today, but it was all very uneventful. The Chester Square house has finally fallen through but, fortunately, we still have the flat. I found that it was most difficult starting to use my hands again although otherwise my use seems to be doing quite nicely. In the evening I had supper at Pat's with Frank and Susan – she used to be a WAAF officer – and Dorothy and David. David is vastly improved since he started to have lessons again. Last week I had lunch with Sidney Holland* who told me that Bill Barlow is planning to take an FRCS and that he, Sidney, is supposed to go through the training course in a year['s time].

Tuesday 18th June

I visited Mrs Gaze this morning. She is very ill but recovering. Alan Murray* joined the training course yesterday. I had tea with Dick and a long, rather unprofitable talk about the work. I am still finding difficulty in using my hands again. In the evening I had a drink with Pat. It seems to be true about Bill.

Wednesday 19th June

The students' class was held in the morning so that FM could go to Ascot. It was a long and rather dull day. I gave two lessons in the afternoon which will probably help me in regaining a better use of my hands. Watts' new pamphlet – a collection of reprints entitled *Knowing How to Stop* is out today: published at 2/6d it seems excellent and should sell vastly.[18]

At night I had dinner at Veglio's with FM, AR, Margaret and Irene. Very enjoyable but nothing notable said or talked of. FM was tired, but AR is a lot better and was in quite excellent form.

Thursday 20th June

This has been another rather uneventful day. I sent off copies of the four books to the Pathfinder Association and then settled down to work with the students. Quite suddenly my co-ordination came back again into my hands, I had more power and assurance in them then at any time since I came back. Pat and I, Dorothy and David lunched together in Chelsea. In class afterwards FM came and helped me whilst working on Dick. He seemed pleased, and truly my co-ordination seemed to be the best yet. Before tea I had a turn from Pip [Ethel Webb*] which struck me as being one of her worst efforts. Afterwards I gave Pilcher a lesson and worked hard on him. In the evening, which I spent at home, I pasted up a lot more sheets of *The Universal Constant*.

Friday 21st June

Rather a miserable sort of day from the point of view of co-ordination. The class was in the morning and then in the course of the day I had Pilcher, Barrington, Gillespie and Lee, which is more teaching than I have had for a week or two. However, Dilys and the children came back in the afternoon so the outlook at home was more cheerful.

Monday 24th June

This was the commencement of what promises to be a very busy week. My use and co-ordination has fortunately improved a good deal so I have been working quite well. Pilcher observed that there is a characteristic Alexander poise and that a lunatic woman once remarked that Duncan Whittaker reminded her of Donat* in *The Citadel*.

In the evening I drank some cider with Pat and Mr Barrington – I wish the latter would consider coming into the training course. Pat had rather a comic letter from Robert Best regarding the family situation. Cecily is staying with us this week.

Tuesday 25th June

I started two new pupils today, i.e. after FM had given them firsts yesterday. Elwell, ex-army, and Mills, ex-POW I think. G. Smith also came. My co-ordination continues to improve happily. FM came in and helped me with Pilcher, which was a good thing because he was going rather 'heavy' on me.

Wednesday 26th June

Another very busy day. I took six pupils and worked with the students too. FM took Pilcher for his lesson and I watched it. In the evening Pat came to dinner and we gave Dilys a good turn.

Thursday 27th June

Once more six pupils today and a great deal of other work. Dorothy and David, and also Neville, came to dinner in the evening.

Friday 28th June

I started well today but was tired but the end of the day when Pilcher came and he foxed me considerably. In the evening Frank Campbell and Joyce came to dinner. We played a lot of music and Frank showed a very intelligent interest in the work.

Monday 1st July

A very hot, tiring day and I had seven pupils. Jean MacInnes was in and worked with the students. FM approved the account forms I printed over the weekend. Pat took Pilcher for me and he went very well, it seems.

Wendy and George came in the evening. The shop is sold at last. The children put water in the tank of the car.

Tuesday 2nd July

Wendy and George were here and I went out with Pat and Dorothy and David to see the *Victory Crazy Show* at the Victoria Palace. It was moderately funny.

I took Pilcher myself and he seemed rather better. That man worries me.

Wednesday 3rd July

Wendy and George returned today but the cider arrived at last – much overdue. Again I took Pilcher but still find him difficult – otherwise I think my teaching improves.

Thursday 4th July

In the morning I took a little woman who was three months pregnant and at the end she fainted on me. She was going very well, too. Benn came in the evening. FM took Pilcher and gave him a good shaking up, but whether this will do any good remains to be seen.

Friday 5th July

This was another very busy day but I seemed to be working fairly well just the same. Pilcher was very depressed and I think he is very difficult for me. However, he has FM on Monday.

Monday 8th July

I had a haircut at 9 o'clock and then took Susan Ladbroke. She is very difficult for she does not seem to have much interest or real understanding of what it is all about. My other pupils were all better and Dorothy Drew gave me a very good turn. Even Crundall seemed to go quite well today. I have not recorded how the other day Mrs Crundall thanked me for her lesson and said that I seemed to have quite a different technique from the other teachers!

FM settled up with me today for last month. I earned £48 in fees and got paid £40 by him with £4 for my share of the teaching, so I haven't done so badly.

Pat came home with me to drink a little cider.

Tuesday 9th July

I had a 9.30 pupil this morning and so started the day well. Then I visited the bank and paid £20 in. At about 11.15 Johnny Anderson turned up to see me. He has a wonderful job with I.C.I. I gave him a *Knowing How to Stop* to read. Ronnie has been back in England for some time. I did a lot of work with the students and Elisabeth said that my hands seemed to have improved a lot lately. We had a good class and then I had a pupil. Pilcher came after tea and was going a little better. FM said he was as heavy as lead. Happily he has now made the connection between this and his heaviness in drawing. Afterwards I watched a Sissons lesson. The good lady who fainted is coming to me again tomorrow. She said she had enjoyed her lesson so much.

In the evening Irene Stewart came to dinner and was very charming. She first had lessons immediately after the last war. She would like to run a guest house in the Highlands. She does not want to share a flat with Margaret Goldie. She told us of her excellent work attending confinements. She once visited Biskara.

Wednesday 10th July

Another long, hot day. I had a 9.30 pupil, a ten o'clock and an eleven, after which I worked with the students. Dorothy Drew did some excellent work on me before lunch which we made in picnic style on the Embankment. After class there was another pupil and then tea, followed by yet another. Finally I wrote letters.

Thursday 11th July

I took Mrs Friswell again and once more she nearly fainted on me but all was well and I think she enjoyed her lesson. After that I had Elwell, followed by Mills and another pupil. I was very hot and tired by the end of the morning. Pat and Dorothy and I had lunch together and then there was the class. After that Pip gave me a turn lasting nearly half-an-hour that did me a lot of good, even if her methods are very rough and ready. She pointed out the value of having the toes turned fairly well out and getting a similar pull on the legs to the one we get with the arms, i.e. keeping the wrists and ankles in.

Later, at tea, we spoke of the evils of building up children's shoes as a cure for fallen arches and FM instanced the case of a famous school where pupils are actually taught to bend their ankles out in order to avoid flat feet. After tea, I took Pilcher and Sissons. The former is showing some signs of improvement, but he is still very heavy. At night Margaret and Jack Fleming came to dinner.

Friday 12th July

This day rather centred round the fact that in class this morning John and Douglass mentioned that Sherrington had referred to the work in his new book. After lunch I bought the book, *The Endeavour of Jean Fernel* and, sure enough, the quotation constitutes recognition from Sherrington at last.[†] FM was tremendously excited. Apart from this, it was the usual sort of day – picnic lunch in the car with Dorothy and Pat, lots of pupils and so on. Dick and Elisabeth came to dinner in the evening.

FM said one very important thing in class. Never to do anything that lowers the standard of your manner of use. It is no good doing something that puts you wrong and then trying to put yourself right in the process. The thing to do is to stop and only to do what you can do without interfering.

Monday 15th July

I took Mr Duff early in the morning, i.e. at 9.30, more or less in a trance. I hate teaching before I have properly woken up. The rest of the morning was largely uneventful. Dorothy, Pat and I lunched together as usual and we had a quiet students' class. After tea, Pilcher came in and had a moderate lesson. It transpires that he is interested in yoga, astrology and mysticism, etc. I am not surprised.

I went home fairly early and George and Wendy arrived to spend the week with us.

Tuesday 16th July

Today I wrote a long letter to Sherrington for FM thanking him for the reference in the book and hoping to interest him in the Jokl case. Afterwards there was the house-warming party at 7 Evelyn Mansions, Margaret Goldie's new flat. We had turkey's eggs and strawberries and cider. Marjory and Bill were there looking amazingly well. McDonagh was there, too, and I had some chat about the Balkans with him. He is very fat and pulled-down now. FM recited as of old. Dorothy drove me home in her car.

[†] This recognition is also quoted in Walter Carrington's pamphlet, 'How We Use Ourselves,' Appendix A, page 67.

Wednesday 17th July

This was a very busy day. I had eight pupils, starting at 9.30 with Elwell. He was doing nicely. There followed the students' class, after which Mr Marshall, a very difficult and interesting case. His manner of use is so distorted that I don't know how he lives. Before lunch I had Mrs Aston.

I lunched with Pat and we got back early and I lay on the floor and had a good turn from Dick until 2.30, when I took Susan. I got on well with her today. After that there was Piggott, also good, and finally Pilcher who is rather better these days. After a quick tea I had Andrews, who is excellent now, and, finally, Mrs Sissons who was more difficult than usual, having been celebrating her husband's examination result last night.

Berrangé arrived from S. Africa today and I take an excellent view of him. He is fortyish in age and much like Lawrence of Arabia to look at. FM was with him all afternoon and evening, and, after my day of teaching, I had a drink and some chat with them. All goes well for the case, but it seems that Jokl arrived in this country last week and, amusing news, the Ling Physical Culture People published excerpts from his *Manpower* article over here last year,[19] without knowing that there was a libel action pending. So we shall be able to have some fun with them: and if they climb down, as they may well do before the S.A. case comes to trial, it will be most damaging to Jokl's defence.

Thursday 18th July

A rather humdrum day with plenty of teaching and hard work. I had about eight pupils again and so was fairly tired by the end of the day.

Friday 19th July

In class this morning FM told us that the conference with the lawyers had gone very well yesterday. Berrangé is pleased with the English Counsel and the English lawyers with him. FM also referred to Robert Nichols,* the poet, who used to come to him as a pupil. He could only work when lying down on the bed in his attic bedroom, smoking Turkish cigarettes. He used to send FM 30-page letters, all in green ink.

I took ten pupils today, my record so far, and did very well on it. In the evening I went with Dilys to *The Mikado* at the King's Theatre, Hammersmith.

Monday 22nd July

I only took seven pupils today but I worked a lot with the students, too, and that kept me sufficiently busy. I had lunch tête-à-tête with Dorothy and she showed me some photographs taken of herself a few years ago. The change is so striking that one would be inclined to think they were fakes. We talked about the difficulties of organising a school for ourselves.

In the evening I was so tired that I went to sleep on the floor listening to the news.

Tuesday 23rd July

My first pupil was at nine this morning, which is much too early. Then I had four in swift succession. I decided then that I did not want to teach any more in the morning. So I went and had a nice browse in the safe instead, under the pretext of digging up things for the case. One treasure I found was the Magnus lectures.[20]

Dorothy, Pat and I had lunch in the sandwich-bar and then rode to the park in the car and ate peaches.

In the class FM told us how Dr Dixon had been in for a lesson yesterday – he did not mention the name – and claimed that he had discovered a lot of new ways of putting the work across, such as instructing to 'stand high', 'stand on half the feet', to 'flatten the back'. When FM had pointed out the error of his ways we went on to point out that what he did when doing what he called 'flattening the back' was the very thing that would bring on the fibrositis and associated condition from which he had been suffering recently. In fact, he had recently disputed a doctor's diagnosis of his condition but FM said that this was because, subconsciously, he knew it was correct. His main trouble arose from too keen a desire to do good and to help people.

I had tea out with Patrick and, after one more lesson, returned home early.

Wednesday 24th July

This was an easier day, although a return of the heat made work fairly unbearable. I taught at ten, ten thirty and twelve thirty. Marshall is doing particularly well. Pat, Dorothy and I had lunch from sandwiches, which we ate in the car.

Berrangé goes by air to Nice tomorrow for a while.

Pat helped me a bit with Pilcher after tea and it was certainly a big help to have both of us working together. I was very tired and so came home early.

Thursday 25th July

This morning I had Mills at 9.30 and he was going fairly well but I find that I have to do quite a bit of work before I am at all 'up' in the mornings and the early lessons are a great strain.

I had lunch with Pat and Dorothy as usual, and during the class FM talked a little about the case. Berrangé is very pleased with the English Counsel. The Commission will not be taken until October because the other side have asked for two and a half months to prepare their case; and they have approached Berrangé after their two moral defeats[21] in court to ask that other preliminaries should be arranged between them instead of going to court again. But Berrangé will be able to see all our evidence prepared before he leaves.

With regard to the Ling people: it appears that Berrangé met a woman official of theirs who is a friend of his in the street a couple of days before he left. She asked him if he had seen the article published in their Journal and offered to give him a copy straight away. The S. African Association strongly disapproved the London Association's action in publishing the article and communicated with them to say so. When he arrived in England, Mr Berrangé went to see the London Editor and found it to be a newly appointed woman. She was most upset about the matter and took it up with her officials, pressing for a retraction and threatening to resign if it were not forthcoming. FM's counsel advised that if the Ling people did not retract there was no alternative but to make them parties to the action and to sue them for £20,000. However, a good letter has been drafted to make it as easy as possible for them to retract and they were holding a meeting this afternoon. One condition is that they must hand over the correspondence with Jokl leading to the publication of the article. It is expected that this will prove to be on official government paper. The joke is that Jokl went to the Ling people the day after Berrangé's visit and so was sent away with a 'flea in his ear'. The Editor was ringing up FM this morning and being very friendly and nice.

After tea I gave Mary Lord a lesson. Then I wrote a letter and came home.

Friday 26th July

The last day of term. I started with two pupils before the class and then had class from 11.30 to 1 pm. After that Tom invited Dorothy, Pat and me out for a small lunch-time session. In the afternoon I was slightly the worse for wear but had recovered in time for my 3.30 pupil. After tea I first had Pilcher, who is going much better, and then FM paid me. In June it seems I cleared £12 over my basic rate – nice work. FM said I was to have full fee for all the work I do in the holiday and next week in the mornings we are going to be very busy indeed, Pat and I. Rumour is that Guy Baron wants to come into the training course in September. Dilys' mother and father came to spend the weekend with us.

Monday 29th July

This morning I took five pupils at N° 16: viz. Johnson, Elwell, Friswell, Pilcher and Mills. Pat was teaching at the same time. Then we went to the Grosvenor to drink to the health of Mr Gould's new baby, who arrived on Saturday with Dorothy and Irene in attendance. After this I had lunch with Pat at his house. Dorothy joined us and we went over to Hampstead to see her mother on whom Pat worked. Dr Pilcher wants to enter the training course and saw FM about it. Sherrington has written a wonderful letter to FM, of which more details later. Mother and Dad returned home.

Tuesday 30th July

Another hard day of work. I took six pupils, starting at 9.30: White, Elwell, Ladbroke, Friswell, Mills and Gould. Then I had lunch with Pat and Dorothy at Pat's, after which we worked on each other until 4.30. When I returned home I took the children and Mother, Dilys and Dad: the latter is going wonderfully. Christopher has developed measles today.

Other news is that the Ling people are retracting, that the S. African Government have paid Brian's training fees, and I saw the Sherrington letter, which is excellent. He says he has long appreciated the value of his [Alexander's] work and is glad now to be able to say so in print: that he sympathises with the difficulties of gaining recognition and he is sorry that he should have been subjected to a scurrilous attack: that Germans are the same the whole world over.

Wednesday 31st July

This morning I took the following pupils: Duff, Barrington, Elwell, Pilcher, Mills and Porter. After that Pat came to lunch at home where Dorothy joined us later and we did some work. Later I also took Dilys, the children, Dad and Mother.

There was no news of any moment, but I should have recorded yesterday that Dorothy remarked adversely on the fact that Dick is to commence teaching in September. She observed that, whereas he is likely to do himself little harm, he may not do much good to others. 'He says to me "now keep that", when he has given me nothing to keep.' Irene Tasker also says he is very heavy. Personally I have not found this so, but it is of some interest.

Thursday 1st August

Six pupils again this morning: White, Elwell, Friswell, Tyler, Pilcher and Mills. It was quite amusing. Tyler, a comic little man, talked all the time without cease and said I have very sensitive hands. Pilcher talked of coming into the training course – he had been accepted – and also invited me to a party in September. Mills had his last lesson today. To my surprise I find he pays full fees – they ought to be double.

After a hasty lunch I went to Lincoln's Inn to meet Haynes and spend the rest of the day with him. At dinner we had sole and chicken and an excellent claret.

Friday 2nd August

This was the lightest day of the week. I only had three pupils: Elwell, Friswell and Pilcher. But after this I had lunch with my Father and Patrick went away for his holiday.

––––––– ❧ –––––––

Monday 9th September

The Autumn Term started today. Dick Walker has now come onto the paid staff. A number of new students have come forward, including Dr Pilcher and Miss Chile Gray,* the school-teacher from Burgess Hill School. Next week we are to have the course divided into two classes and to move over to Goldie's flat. There was the usual bustle and muddle on the first day. I only gave one lesson and found it hard to get back to teaching form. There is no doubt that I need the stimulus of having to teach to keep me up to the standard of co-ordination necessary; but I think the same is true of FM. Duncan Whittaker is joining the course this term too – which is indeed news.

In the evening we went over to Hampstead for dinner with Marjory and Bill. The latter has just been appointed Medical Registrar at the Ratcliffe and promised a job later as assistant to the Professor of Social Medicine at the University. I told them that Charles and Eric are now advertising that they are back at work and ready to teach the Technique outlined in the books etc. This caused much amusement. Bill told a number of stories of FM's recent visit to France,[22] which were quite interesting but not worth repetition here. He also told us that Berrangé is way over to the Left in politics – disturbing news in a way, for we do not want the work to have a leftist bias. Later they drove us home in their car.

Tuesday 10th September

Another very quiet day at Ashley Place. In the evening Pat and I had a few drinks at the Duke of Wellington and then we went on to his place for supper with the Ladbrokes, where Dilys joined us. At lunch-time we discussed a new restaurant in Victoria.

Wednesday 11th September

Ronnie Milson turned up for lunch and I took him to the little restaurant where we had a very interesting chat about old times.

In the evening FM and Margaret came out to dinner. We had a lovely evening, not once talking shop but all of his experiences in France, and so on. In class I remarked that I seemed to have a tricky pull on the left side of my neck. He said it was nothing much but that we all have to watch ourselves: even he had caught himself up to tricks since he caught this recent germ on returning from France. He said it in such a kindly way that I was very touched.

Thursday 12th September

I worked hard with the students and it appears that we shall have some entertainment about psychiatry with all these psychiatrists in the class.[23]

FM is in much better condition today and I watched him give a brilliant lesson to Marshall. In the evening Sidney Holland came to me for a lesson. He is having difficulty in finding time to attend the students' class properly. Finally Jim and his wife Phyl came. I introduced them to FM who felt Jim's back and said that he could be much helped. Then I took them home to dinner and we had a very pleasant evening of chat about nothing much.

Friday 13th September

This was a very interesting day. I worked hard as usual with the students in the morning and part of the afternoon. Then I watched FM interview a woman who had an iron on her leg and trouble in walking. The question was: could she be made to see that her trouble was caused, not by Nature, but her own doing and would she admit that she had the power to inhibit, for instance, the desire to walk. He worked on her and talked to her for half an hour, at the end of which she was practically in tears, but I think he had carried his point. Later, I gave what I thought to be one of the best lessons I have ever given to Skinner.

In the evening Irene Tasker came to dinner and we talked over all the old problems of the training course, the School and so on. I find her almost entirely in agreement with my views. She does not think the students get a fair deal and she favours apprenticeships as a means of training rather than a course. She advocates discussion groups of small numbers, the writing of papers and so on. The publication of a magazine has been suggested for January. She advises me to dig my heels in and have nothing to do with it at all. She also agrees that Jokl is sure to try and use Charles Neil and Eric de Peyer in the case.

Sunday 15th September

I telephoned Irene tonight and she says that her favourite niece has just visited her and expressed the desire to settle with her when she comes out of the Army. This being so, she may be prepared to settle in S. Africa after all. She will not know the situation, of course, until she has been out there for a bit but, if she does decide to stay, she would ask nothing better than to have me go out and help her. She thinks I am working on the right lines and understands that I must do all I can for FM but, if anything unexpected happened and the situation over here became such that I should want to get away, South Africa would be there!

The weeks Monday 16th to Monday 30th September

This was a very full time, during which I regret that my regular habit of entering in this diary lapsed. On Monday we spent a jolly evening at the Hungeria with Ronnie Milson and his wife, the Andersons and a friend. On Tuesday we had a quiet evening to ourselves. On Wednesday Nellie Robinson came to stay the night. On Thursday the Milsons and Andersons visited us. On Friday I set about some printing for FM – Penhill letterheads. On Saturday Pat came to tea and supper. On Sunday I visited Haynes (22nd).

The following week was a little quieter. On Monday and Tuesday I printed, on Wednesday I went out and drank a little sherry with Pat, Max [Alexander*] the Drews and others. On Thursday we listened to *ITMA* quietly.[24] On Friday we did nothing much but go to bed early. On Saturday we had a great children's party for Christopher which was attended by the Barlow children, the Walker children, Anne Whittaker, Hamish Morrison and Susan Ladbroke, complete with respective parents. Pat came too and stayed to supper. On Sunday I took the children to Church, but lazed most of the rest of the day.

During this week a number of items emerged in connection with the work that ought to be recorded. The following being all that I can salvage from the lumber-rooms of memory. The woman, Miss Carlton, referred to under September 13th, was handed over to Pat and me to work on jointly and she has made most wonderful progress so that she is in a fair way to regaining the use of her injured hand and arm, and walking normally. Dorothy's father, who injured his leg recently, came to FM for lessons on crutches and, in a very short space of time, was walking almost normally with only the aid of a stick. Maxwell is to come on the teaching staff from the first of October. Professor Dart,* Dean of the Medical Faculty of Witwatersrandt University, Johannesburg, has written two good articles for British scientific papers in support of the work. In one he makes reference to Mungo Douglas' paper.[25] Pat tells me that his father first came to FM at his mother's instigation. Mrs Macdonald had been reading *MSI*.

FM gave us some of the story about Coghill, as follows: When he visited him he was a very sick man, half paralysed, dragging one foot after him and living in conditions of extreme poverty in a little two room shack of his own building in Florida.

He was being looked after by his daughter, who lived in a small outbuilding. The walls of one room of the shack were covered from top to bottom with stacks of drawers containing all his scientific records.

In about 1936, Coghill was being hailed as one of the most important men in America. Sponsored by the Macy Foundation, his work was to afford the biologic background for their psychological theories but, when he came out with his endorsement of FM's work,[26] the scientific world dropped him like a red-hot brick. At the same time, he had the misfortune to incur the enmity of the head of the Wistar Institute, with the result that he returned from a holiday to find himself dismissed from his office and all his papers, books, etc., were dumped at his back door out in the open. Although he wrote personally to all the members of the Committee, and to other leading Philadelphians, and asked for a public hearing of his case, he never so much as got an answer to his letters. He was thus left quite without means of support or livelihood, a ruined and broken man.

But, by chance, some relative of his died at this juncture so that he was left sufficient money to buy this small plot of land in a poor quarter of Gainesville, Florida, and to build his humble shack upon it. He was a broken man, yet when FM visited him he was one of the best pupils he ever had, for he seized on the significance of what was being done immediately. Unfortunately FM could not stay long but had to return to New York.

At that time he and his party had very little money since they had only just arrived. They wanted Coghill to go to New York to join them for lessons but, to this end, it was necessary to raise funds to pay for his hotel bill. Accordingly, FM appealed to all his friends (excepting the Blacks, who were away) but not one of them offered a penny, except one lady, almost a stranger, who offered $150. However, Coghill was already a sick man and he had a stroke and was taken to hospital, where he died before the projected visit could be arranged.

He once said to FM that of all the things that most weighed on him was the reflection that he, as a healthy young man, had devoted his life to science and had, by poring over a microscope, discovered these principles and yet been ruined in health whereas FM, as an ailing youth, had looked in a mirror and discovered the same principles and used them to become what he is today.

Coghill never got much help for his researches. He was very poor and even learnt to mend the family shoes so that the money so saved could be used to buy him the instruments he needed. The Wistar Institute once got a substantial grant from the Macy Foundation for the furtherance of his work but he personally never saw a penny of it. Such was the story of Coghill.

Monday 30th September

Today FM was ill. He had been ill all the weekend with a sort of nettle-rash, only something far worse, that gave rise to blotches under the surface of the skin about the size of sixpences all over his body. Very painful and sore. He was in bed all day but got up in the evening to go down to Penhill. Irene also was not well today, having a bad headache.

I taught four pupils in the morning and three in the afternoon, also helping Pat with Miss Carlton, as usual, and doing two hours' work with the students. In the morning Pat and I took the students over at the flat, but in the afternoon at $N^{\underline{o}}$ 16. Pat and I lunched together with Maxwell at the usual place.

I was very tired at night, for no particular reason, and so after listening on the wireless to the first part of the judgment on the Nuremberg trial, retired early to bed.

Max started teaching today.

Tuesday 1st October

This day passed much as usual with plenty of work to do and few idle moments.

Thomas Pilcher came to dinner in the evening and we had a lot of interesting talk. He is thoroughly happy and enjoying the training course. Dilys remarked afterwards that it was obvious that he entertained a very high regard for me. He made one interesting point: that the scientific nature of the Technique could not be questioned by anyone who had read the first chapter of *The Use of the Self*.

Wednesday 2nd October

This has been a full and busy day. My teaching goes well but I do get tired. Miss Carlton improves at a wonderful rate that gives us great confidence in our ability to tackle difficult people. There is nothing of unusual interest to report. I finished early at five-thirty and so returned to pass a quiet evening at home.

Thursday 3rd October

FM returned today, not to take pupils, but just the students. He seemed much better. I took Mr Drew, who seemed to be going nicely and, with Pat, Miss Carlton who is also doing well. I was less tired today and derived great benefit from a few minutes work from FM.

Friday 4th October

I gave Miss Hamilton her last lesson before she returned to Glasgow and she was going very well – a great improvement on her first lesson this time when she went off into floods of tears. Bosley was as tricky as ever, but the others were doing well. FM took the students again but nothing happened today of special note. I finished after tea and so came home early.

Monday 7th October

This morning I had a haircut and then went to see my new suit at Gunn, Collie & Todd. FM was in great form in the class. He commenced by castigating Churchill and all demagogues, whom he said talked like gramophones, and quoted Lloyd George's remark that he never took any notice of anything a man said when standing on his feet. He said that the real danger was that a man who could sway a mob could do so as well for evil as for good. From this he passed on to the dangers of music as a stimulus to the instinctive faculties of Man, and so on to Schopenhauer, Nietzsche and Wagner.[27]

After lunch, at the usual place and in the usual company, I went back and worked with the students. Dorothy then made some interesting remarks. Constipation often brings on asthma; but constipation can be caused by a lifting of the chest. Hence a laxative is often a temporary cure for an asthmatic attack. She described current anatomy as largely 'balls and balderdash', as being derived from the study of corpses instead of the living organism.

After tea, Pat, Dorothy and I came home to collect my cider barrel in order that Pat might have it for the party tomorrow. On the way Dorothy told of a woman who consulted her last Saturday night, her trouble being a frequently recurring urge to murder her six-weeks old baby when feeding him. Dorothy diagnosed this as being due to the manner in which she pulled herself down to feed the child. Subsequent experiment and demonstration proved that the urge quite disappeared when Dorothy took her head up and prevented her from pulling down in this way. Dorothy remarked that such cases are by no means uncommon, but quite often result in the murder of the child.

This evening Margot is coming to stay with us for a few days.

Tuesday 8th October

Pat's oyster party today. I did the usual work at Ashley Place and the Cambridge University Press sent their permission for the use of the Sherrington extract: so that is now to print.

In the evening I went with Max to the Sherry bar where Elisabeth joined us and then we all went on to Pat's and ate a great quantity of oysters. Present were Dilys and Dad, Dorothy and David, Elizabeth and Max, Frank and Susan, Elisabeth and Dick, Guy and Tom, Irene Tasker and Sidney Holland, and Patrick. We had a beautiful time.

In the afternoon Pat and I took Mr Bosley together and gave him a good 'smartening up'.

Wednesday 9th October

My day started with Lindwall, who was inclined to be tricky. Then Bosley came along in great form and went awfully well, to my surprise. I had a nice letter from Lili Hellstenius,* all about how she is trying to get FM the Nobel Peace Prize. We had lunch at Pat's to finish off the oysters. In the afternoon I did some of my very best work for the last few weeks, with the students.

After tea, Haycock had a brilliant lesson from FM. I swelled with pride because he is, and has been, very tricky but FM considered he had done very well with the lessons he has had. FM's teaching is so wonderfully simple now, it is a joy to watch him give a lesson. He said it took him a long time to find out why people pulled down after he had got them up out of themselves in a lesson. The answer being that they tried to keep length by stiffening the neck.

Thursday 10th October

This morning I put in some hard work on the students, particularly to try and make Tom say some whispered *ah*'s. In the afternoon, Pat and I set about Brigadier Stevens jointly, to his great good. Duncan Whittaker told me an amusing story of Bosley's reaction to our joint assault last week – how he complained that, with both of us, he could do none of the things he had been able to do before.

In the evening, FM called me in and gave me the little blind girl who is likely to be rather difficult. After work was over Pat and I went and drank some sherry together.

Friday 11th October

The students' class was in the morning to enable FM to go to Ascot. I had lunch with Irene Stewart and her sister-in-law at our usual restaurant. Afterwards I gave a first lesson to the little blind girl – whom I think may be a bit difficult. Tea out with Pat and Dorothy was enlivened by the latter's story of an argument with Pilcher regarding rheumatism and manner of use. P. said 'but rheumatism is a *disease*'.

Monday 14th October

At lunch today Dorothy dropped rather a bomb-shell – news from her father that he was shocked by the size of the FM's bill, could not afford it, etc. and did not consider the 'treatment' had done his leg any good – the shocking old liar.

I had a hardish day's work but was amused by the fact that, although I have almost my full quota of pupils, FM insisted on giving me another after tea. It was purely an accident I think. At night I did a little printing for the family. FM was pleased with Bosley.

Tuesday 15th October

Dilys and the children came up to town for lunch. I worked away much as usual and little out of the ordinary occurred. Miss Boyd, my little blind girl, is doing quite well.

My new suit came from Collie & Todd and was much admired. Renée Tickell rang up after all these years and invited us to tea on Sunday. I printed all the evening for Dad. Pat was not feeling too well this evening.

Wednesday 16th October

Pat was not well today so I had to take some of his pupils for him. I had lunch by myself and afterwards worked in the class. FM took Stevens and Haycock for me and gave the former a great calling over the coals. Later he explained to me that he could feel he thought he was going like a house on fire when he put his hands on him, and he was too, but that was due to the work that had been done on him rather than to his own directing and that would be no good to him later on so he had to get after him. Later I took Bosley, who was doing well, and one of Pat's pupils. I had a drink with Dick before returning home.

Thursday 17th October

Pat was back again today so things went normally. I took Stevens in the morning and gave him a good 'going-over' on the subject of direction. I think I begin to understand the matter better myself. Belinda Peacy came to dinner.

Friday 18th October

Marshall had his last lesson this morning and seemed to do quite well. FM was in terrific form in class, speaking of astrology and Sir Henry Irving and the nature of Reality which he believes to be 'change'. I was very tired, possibly due to changes in myself.

After Miss Carlton's lesson I left early and took the printing rollers to Hunter-Penrose.

In the evening I took Dilys up to Veglio's for dinner.

Monday 21st October

Very Monday-morningish this morning. Haycock, my nine-thirty pupil, was difficult and much pulled down. I saw FM briefly and he told me that one of the medical papers had at last decided to publish something that they had been considering for six months, but which he considered more important than anything else to date.[28]

I had a quiet lunch followed by a quiet class. During Miss Boyd's lesson I was very sleepy but she is doing excellently well. We worked on Miss Carlton for nearly an hour, Pat and I, but after that I had no more teaching to do and so decided to return home.

Tuesday 22nd October

This morning I saw the retraction and apology published by the Ling people in their journal last July.[†] Watts also have a full column advertisement for the books in their weekly edition of the *Manchester Guardian*. FM saw Miss Boyd today and thought she was going well.

In class I worked on Dorothy and found her as slippery as an eel. When I came back from lunch I met her on the stair and she said I had done great harm to her and she thought I ought to know! I forgot to reply: what about the harm she had done to me! Anyway, I must talk to her seriously about it – or perhaps she is having a 'hate' session: but if so, what have I done?

FM and AR both worked on Miss Carlton this afternoon. Later I took Mr Frischaur for Dick and found him very pleasant and interesting. Finally, Pat and I left together in search of beer but could only find a poor pint at the Antelope – Poppa Loom's was shut.

[†] The retraction is quoted in note no. 19, page 81.

Wednesday 23rd October

Dorothy seemed much like herself today so perhaps it was only a 'hate' session. Dilys and I had dinner with Margaret at their flat and then went on to the cinema to see *Une Femme de Boulanger*. FM came with us and enjoyed it immensely.

Thursday 24th October

We had dinner with Wing Commander and Mrs Russell and passed a very pleasant evening with them. They did not make any remarks about the work at all.

Friday 25th October

Pat and I went in the evening to the Pathfinder Club where Charles joined us. Later we all came home for supper pretty 'high' and drank a nice drop of cider. It was an amusing evening but I am not sure how far I trust Charles.

Saturday 26th – Sunday 27th October

Dick Tutton and Madeleine came for the weekend and so all work was suspended but we had a most delightful time. We all went to the cinema on Saturday evening to see a tough film, *The Long Sleep,* and on Sunday lunch-time I took them to The Doves. Dick is much interested in the work.

Monday 28th October

Guy wants me to fly again and pilot a charter aircraft for us all to spend the day in Dublin. I watched FM give Mr Haycock an interesting lesson. He remarked that if he had cared to do it, it would have been so easy for him to make a fortune in five years in the old days. If you tell pupils they are doing well they think you are a wonderful teacher.

Tuesday 29th October

Apparently the 'other side' in the case are presenting a petition to take evidence from the President of the Royal College of Physicians, the President of the Royal College of Surgeons, the

President of the Royal Society, a distinguished physiologist and eight other doctors.[29] Such fun!

I had a quiet day of fairly hard work, taking seven pupils, and then returned home early, being rather tired after my past week of riotous living.

Wednesday 30th October

This morning I did not have to be in until ten o'clock and it is surprising how much difference an extra half-hour makes. We had a very bad and late lunch. The service was abominable, largely, I think, because the people there do not like Dorothy. In the class we listened to the Cambridgeshire Handicap. Pat took his father to see FM last night with regard to the petition. After work was over Pat and I had a drink at the Sherry Bar.

Thursday 31st October

A most satisfactory sort of day. All my pupils went well and I did some good work. Mungo Douglas' article on Experimental Verification was published today in *The Medical Press and Circular*. I had lunch by myself at our usual restaurant and received excellent attention and service. Pat tells me that FM is still an undischarged bankrupt.[30] A funny little South African man asked today to have all his lessons from me and flattered me into giving him a nine o'clock appointment in the morning. [Colonel] Shaw had a lesson from FM after tea and did extremely well, which, of course, does not do my reputation any harm. Elisabeth Walker did some very good work on me at tea-time. She will make a fine teacher one day, I think.

Friday 1st November

Hallis was late for his nine o'clock appointment which rather annoyed me. But Haycock did well and so did Carlton. Afterwards I had Mrs Macdonald, whom I think is a dear, kindly person, and she spoke of her anxiety for Pat. After this I worked with the students for a little and then took White, who seems to be doing well now. Pat and I had lunch as usual, and an excellent lunch too.

The class in the afternoon was productive of an interesting story with regard to the Tic Douloureux case.[31] Shepherd, a surgeon friend of Murdoch's, was sympathetic and interested in the work but had never met FM. When he heard of the T.D. case he said, 'Alexander has made a big mistake to attempt anything with that because I am a specialist in it and the trigeminal ganglion is shredded and I don't see how change in manner of use can possibly affect that.' However, of course, the trouble did disappear and when he met FM afterwards he spoke about it. FM said: 'Well, have you read Caldwell's* letter?' and he said, 'Why yes, that was what first attracted me to your work.' 'Could it not be then', said FM, 'that much the same thing is taking place in this case as in the other – some reflex spasm is responsible for the shredding of the ganglion and when that is inhibited the ganglion grows again!' Shepherd replied, 'Why yes, that is the first theory I have ever heard put forward that I would be prepared to entertain.'

FM then went on to tell how Spicer had called him up after reading the first reports of Pavlov's work and said, 'Here is a man who has done something years ahead of your work. I must see you at once to give you all the particulars about it.' FM said, 'If that is so I must hear about it at once so that I can go to him and work with him.' After dinner Spicer started to read out and explain the report on Pavlov and FM began to laugh, saying, 'Why that is what we have been doing with circus animals for years.' Spicer looked very serious and then he began to laugh too. At that moment his wife came in and so they explained the matter to her and she said, 'How like you, Scanes, to allow yourself to be taken in by a Russian of all people.'

After class I took Dr Leishman, who seems to be doing quite nicely, and then Brigadier Stevens, who continues to make excellent progress. That was all my work for the day, so I returned home early to prepare for our dinner guests. W/Commander and Mrs Russell came to dinner and we had a very enjoyable evening, talking of not very much and drinking a fair amount of cider. If I could have foreseen three years ago when I first met him that I should be entertaining him and his wife in my own home so soon how much happier I should have been.

Monday 4th November

I was very tired this morning after my day with Haynes yesterday. Haycock was going fairly well and afterwards I had John Gosse, who is now doing a two-year photographic course at Blackpool. He is much improved, both in speaking and general manner of use. Next came Carlton and Boyd – both doing quite nicely. Pat, Dorothy, Douglass and I had lunch of sandwiches and grapes on the Embankment in the car. A new student came in today, Mr Skinner,* an Australian W.D. Air-gunner who was prisoner of the Japs for three and a half years. Otherwise the class was uneventful. Afterwards I took Dr Leishman and friend Bosley, who turned up again doing quite well.

At tea FM said that he had, at last, decided that we must cut out in future teaching all instructions to order the neck to relax or to be free because such orders only lead to other forms of doing. If a person is stiffening the neck, the remedy is to get them to stop projecting the messages that are bringing about this condition and not to project messages to counteract the effects of the other messages. He said that the implied contradiction had worried him for a long time but, after working on Hallis this morning, he saw that it must be changed so all orders in future will be framed so as to emphasise 'non-doing'.

After this I gave Shaw a good lesson and then Stevens. Finally I had a drink with Dick on the way home. Aunty Alice was staying the night which rather hindered work in the evening, but I was too tired anyway.

Tuesday 5th November

John Gosse did quite well this morning and so did Miss Carlton. Afterwards I helped FM with a new pupil, a Mr Westlake (I think), who promises to be very difficult. The class was un-eventful. I had lunch with Max and told him the story of FM's bankruptcy which he had never heard before. Afterwards I had a haircut.

Working with the students, later, we had some amusement in talking to Pilcher about various forms of madness. Then I had Scott and Bosley before tea. Afterwards there was Shaw and Kinton. I discovered, to my horror, that, although the latter has had about 30 lessons (mostly from Dick), he had never been taken on the table before and only done whispered *ah*'s once previously.

That was the end of the day and I had to return home early to let off fireworks for the children.

Wednesday 6th November

Pat, Dorothy, David, Felicity, Dilys and I went to see the Marx Bros. at Notting Hill Gate.

Thursday 7th November

I returned home fairly early and we had a quiet evening doing very little.

Friday 8th November

Haycock came in the morning and seemed a little easier. He wants to end his lessons soon. Stevens is going so well that I have now cut him down to once a week. Bosley had his last lesson today – so I shall soon be short of pupils.

I visited the dentist, Eric Pedley, after tea. He could only find one minute hole and says that the children's teeth should be very good. Later I took Dilys to see the Australian film, *The Overlanders* and we had supper at The Doves.

Monday 11th November

This morning I went in fairly late to take Miss Carlton. She had a very good lesson, going a great deal better than she has done for a long time. After that I had Miss Boyd, who continues to go well, and then there was the students' class.

The other afternoon in class FM spoke of his first meeting with Sir Henry Irving. When he arrived in this country it was his great ambition to meet Sir Henry, but rather than seek him out without introduction he preferred to wait until an invitation should come to him. One day William, his old servant who had an aunt on the stage, came into his room with a single letter on the silver tray, saying, 'A letter for you, sir, that you will be delighted to receive – it's from Sir Henry – I'd know that writing anywhere.'

After the class I had White who seems to be going well but is still doing his best to feel it all out. For lunch I went with Pat and Dorothy and Douglass to the Polish restaurant where we had quite a good meal. After lunch I worked with the students and then Pat and I took Scott jointly and gave him a very good lesson. Before tea I had Westlake, who is making steady progress.

At tea-time FM had a letter from Professor Raymond Dart that he read out to us. The article on malocclusion has been published in *The Journal of the Dental Association of South Africa*. There is no news yet of the one for the *Bulletin of Royal College of Surgeons*.[32]

After tea I wrote some letters for Irene and there was nothing more so I returned and spent a quiet evening at home. Wendy is staying with us while George attends a Civil Service Selection Board for a couple of nights.

Tuesday 12th November

This morning I had Miss Boyd at ten o'clock and gave her a good turn on the couch. Carlton did not come because of the crowds due to the opening of Parliament. Stevens had a very good lesson again. I think he is nearly finished now, so to speak. I worked with the students after this and then had Miss Aspiden for half an hour. She is very tricky but quite interesting. Pat and I had lunch at the old restaurant together, and a very good lunch too.

In class FM was speaking of Roman Catholics, religion in general, and Sandow* and the physical culturists. He remarked on how difficult, in general, RCs were to teach. Then he remarked on how, during the time that Maurice Baring was coming for lessons, he was visited by a little RC priest who had obviously come to check up on what Baring was doing. Once, he said, a priest visited him and said that whilst he could not come for lessons, he thought he might like to know that there was nothing in his books to which RCs could object. When Methuen's readers advised against publishing *MSI*, although FM was to pay for it himself, the head of the firm sent it to Professor Frank Granger,* the nonconformist divine. He not only approved it in glowing terms, but even came up from Nottingham to see FM and congratulate him on it.

With regard to Sandow, FM said that he had known his great friend who was responsible for launching him on his public career by encouraging him to accept a challenge at some music hall to pick up a horse with a man on it. Sandow was an unintelligent but extremely strong man. This event, with its subsequent publicity, attracted the attention of some people who signed him up to a contract and faked up the whole thing for him, although he had never done an exercise in his life. He made vast sums of money and cultivated enormous varicose veins all over himself by doing his exercises. All the Bishops and Cabinet Ministers flocked to him.

Before tea I had Scott and Westlake – both of whom did reasonably well. After tea Fred Watts was in for a lesson. He said that now at last all the books were in stock and he was launching a big advertising campaign. A number of papers refused *Knowing How to Stop* as being associated in their minds with cures for masturbation. *The Times* also would not accept advertisements including Sir Stafford Cripps' testimonial. The books are selling well and the paper situation is easier. Carlton's father had been to see him and asked him to pass on the information that his daughter had had an operation to remove a large clot of blood from her brain and she does not know anything about this.

I had no more work to do and so came home early to spend another quiet evening.

Wednesday 13th November

I went in latish to take Miss Boyd – she can now see the hands of a clock – followed by Carlton and Westlake. The former was shaking steadily, although her head was more free than I have ever known it before.

In class FM spoke about the scientific nature of the Technique, how each step leads inevitably to the next so that the immediate end, once achieved, is only the means to the next end so, he says, should be our means-whereby for living. Incidentally he said that if humanity had idolised the acrobat rather than the athlete there might be a vastly different story to tell because the latter is always 'undoing' to gain his ends and thus tends always to have a high standard of use and co-ordination.

I had lunch alone and then went to work with the students. Dorothy complained to Dick that by taking her head he had done her a lot of harm. I was much amused by this, especially after my own experience in the matter recently. An amicable discussion followed in which I think Dorothy carried her point very well. Haycock had a very good lesson, first from FM and then from me. FM went over much of the same ground with him that he covered with the students in the morning. Mr Piggott came in before tea with a copy of P. Boomer's book *On Learning Golf* that contains a lot about FM and nearly all utterly perverted.[33] As FM said, anybody can get marvellous results by not teaching this Technique. Elizabeth Alexander brought Max's baby into tea – a nice little thing. Afterwards I did some nice work with Pat, and Dick watched.

Thursday 14th November

This morning I took Mrs Carmichael first. A woman who runs her home and looks after four children and yet manages to improve since her first lot of lessons three years ago. She comes up periodically for a refresher course. Carlton was tricky again; and Gillespie, whom I have not taken for a long time, much better but dull. Boyd had an excellent lesson from FM which I watched. Pat and I lunched together quietly and alone at the New Continental. Nothing very much emerged in class. Scott had quite a good lesson from me, and Stevens an excellent one from FM which I watched.

After tea I took J. Murray for Dick. He was going quite nicely, but he had had 30 lessons and not done whispered *ah*'s before! To finish off the day, Pat and I went and had a most enjoyable little session at the Pathfinders.

Friday 15th November

Beryl continues to go well and Carlton was much better again. Then I had a Mrs Mitchell who has a back, much what Dilys's used to be. In the students' class there was much talk about flying and they made me repeat my experiences in doing a parachute jump. Pat and I lunched together.

Then, in afternoon class, only Dorothy and Peter Scott turned up so Dick and I took one each. We talked of the way in which misuse develops until a point is reached where the slightest stimulus is sufficient to produce major symptoms – e.g. blackout.

Pat and I took Westlake together and gave him a good 'doing'. I saw the end of Scott's lesson and FM reported him doing excellently. He, Scott, remarked to me as he was leaving, 'Tell Pat that I saw his father in the Club last night. He was sitting up wonderfully all the evening. He never forgot. He looked *damned miserable,* but he never forgot.'

I worked with the students again until tea-time and then waited about to take Dr Leishman at 5.30. He was late and so I was also. He remarked on the great problem of putting this work across in medical circles and asked whether I thought that FM's work was personal genius or could be transmitted. I don't think he realised how rude the question was until I alluded to it! Pat thinks he is probably toying with the notion of the training course.

Pat's father reports that the President of the Royal College of Surgeons (whose name I cannot recall at the moment) is willing to give evidence that he considers FM a 'quack', on the grounds that his books might lead people to attempt non-recognised forms of treatment where proper medical advice is required.

───────── ❧ ─────────

This marks the end of the 1946 diary. A further, single entry was made the following year on the occasion of Walter Carrington's overhearing Alexander talking about his youth.

Tuesday 30th September 1947

This afternoon, whilst giving a lesson to Mr Wint,* FM gave the fullest account of his early life that I have ever heard.

He said that, as a boy, he went to school in Tasmania but was, from the first, a most awkward and difficult pupil because of his reluctance to take information on trust and to submit to the usual school routine. Eventually the schoolmaster, rather an unusual Scotsman of good family who had gone out there for reasons of health, saw his father and arranged to give him special private tuition in the evening. This was all the regular schooling he ever got and, in return, he would win all the prizes and awards for the school whenever called upon to do so. Doing examinations came very naturally and easily to him. When the time came for him to leave school, his master wanted him to go on to train for the teaching profession but he was also offered a job with the Mount Bischoff Tin-Mining Company at a salary of two pounds, ten shillings a week – unheard of pay for a youngster beginning a job in those days. After much thought he decided to take the job and one of the hardest things he ever had to do in his life was to inform his schoolmaster, Robertson, of his decision. He said that after he had broken the news to him they both sat in silence for a quarter of an hour.

However, at the Tin-Mining Company, all went well. Within a fortnight he found himself doing highly responsible work, owing to the illness of his boss, and his efforts were so much appreciated that he was paid a special bonus. About this time, he undertook an insurance agency at the usual commission of one pound per cent, and it is related that when the chief of the company signed a two thousand pound policy with him he went skipping out of the room. It was the first twenty pounds that he had ever earned. Later he also undertook, by tender, special book-keeping work for the company, being appointed in spite of the fact that his tender was nearly three times as much as the others.

After three years with the company he had saved quite a sum of money so he resigned, in spite of protests, and returned to Melbourne. Here he went on a glorious spree whilst his funds lasted, visiting all sorts of entertainments (Sarah Bernhardt was making her Australian tour and he went to see her twice a day whilst she was in Melbourne), buying the best of clothes, and so on.

After this he began to look around for another job. His uncle warned him that this would not be easy in Melbourne where he was unknown, but he answered three advertisements, attended three interviews and, in course of time, had the choice of all three jobs. He took one with a firm of estate agents, but only remained happy in it for three months. Thereafter he had a number of different jobs, always managing to rise and improve his position and prospects.

Meanwhile he was keeping on with his dramatic reciting, which he had first taken to at the age of six as the birds sing, and eventually he decided to undertake this professionally. He gave up his work and embarked on a six months' tour of New Zealand.

Before this was over he had been offered a most tempting engagement in America but he had already decided to try and see if he could teach his technique and so turned it down. At the end of his tour he announced that he would stay on and teach in Auckland for three or four months before going back to Melbourne and almost immediately he had more pupils than he could take, including the Mayor of Auckland and many other worthies.

Subsequently he returned to Australia and said that the next two or three years, whilst he sought to establish himself, were the most difficult years of his life. He was then between twenty-three and twenty-six years of age and, of course, all his family thought him quite mad.

When his first success with the Mount Bischoff Tin-Mining Company was recognised he was invited to a big company dinner, but at first refused under the plea that he had promised his mother not to smoke or drink. The head of the firm, however, refused to accept this excuse and undertook to write to his mother to get her permission. After this, of course, he attended the dinner and care was taken by certain bright sparks to see that his glass was constantly filled. Just the same, it is related that he and one of the senior members of the firm who was a friend of his, were the only two that were able to find their way to bed that night unaided and they walked to the top of the mountain together first.

———— ❧ ————

HOW WE USE OURSELVES

WHEN Mr. Alexander started the experiments described in *The Use of the Self** he was trying to find out what he *did* in using his voice that caused trouble with his throat. He soon came to realize that "we do not *know* how we use ourselves any more than the dog or cat *knows*." But as, by experience, he gained something of this knowledge, he saw that "in the process of acquiring a conscious direction of the use of the human organism a hitherto 'undiscovered country' is opened up, where the scope for the development of human potentialities is practically unlimited, and anyone who chooses to take the time and trouble to carry out the procedures necessary for acquiring a conscious direction of use can put this to the test."

Sir Charles Sherrington, the great authority on the brain and nervous system, has summed up this problem *of knowing how we use ourselves* in the following passage from his book *The Endeavour of Jean Fernel*† :

"The more primitive animals are less mentalized, and these, where there is a nervous system, manage to live mainly by 'reflex' action. Their quota of mentalized behaviour is relatively small, and in some instances vanishingly so. Descended from a long stock of less mentalized creatures as we are, and living less reflexly than did they, our more mentalized status has arrived at putting the reflex mechanism as a going concern, within the control, to a certain extent, of the reactions of the brain. This mastery of the brain

---

*F. MATTHIAS ALEXANDER: *The Use of the Self*. Chaterson Ltd. London, 1946. (Third Edition.)

†SIR CHARLES SHERRINGTON, O.M.: *The Endeavour of Jean Fernel* Cambridge University Press. 1946. Pps. 88-89. Extract reproduced with the permission of the Publishers.

over the reflex machinary does not take the form of inter-meddling with reflex details; rather it dictates to a reflex mechanism 'you may act' or 'you may not act.' The detailed execution of the motor act is still in immediate charge of the reflex. Our individual history exemplifies this. A child late in 'learning to walk', which has perhaps never yet walked, will unexpectedly get up and walk passably well. Its walk-ing has come to it as part of its growth; its mind simply had not earlier given it the cue. One of Shakespeare's characters exclaims, 'Mind is the slave of life'. That is profoundly so; but of all life's slaves, mind, though the most enlightened, is the most prone to truant.

It is largely the reflex element in the willed movement or posture which, by reason of its unconscious character, de-feats our attempts to know the 'how' of the doing of even a willed act. Breathing, standing, walking, sitting, although innate, along with our growth, are apt, as movements, to suffer from defects in our ways of doing them. A chair un-suited to a child can quickly induce special and bad habits of sitting, and of breathing. In urbanized and industrialized communities bad habits in our motor acts are especially common. But verbal instructions as to how to correct wrong habits of movement and posture is very difficult. The scant-iness of our sensory perception of how we do them makes it so. The faults tend to escape our direct observation and recognition. Of the proprioceptive reflexes as such, whether of muscle or ear (vestibule), we are unconscious. We have no direct perception of the 'wash' of the labyrinthine fluid, or, indeed, of the existence of the labyrinths at all. In their case subjective projection, instead of indicating, blinds the place of their objective source. Correcting the movements carried out by our proprioceptive reflexes is something like trying to reset a machine, whose works are intangible, and the net output all we know of the running. Instruction in such an act has to fall back on other factors more accessible to sense; thus, in skating, to 'feeling' that edge of the skate-blade on which the movement bears. To watch another performer trying the movement can be helpful; or a looking-glass in which to watch ourselves trying it. The mirror can tell us often more than can the most painstaking attempt to 'introspect'. Mr. Alexander has done a service* to the subject by insistently treating each act as involving the whole integrated individual, the whole psycho-physical man. To take a step is an affair, not of this or that limb solely, but of the total neuro-muscular activity of the moment—not least of the head and the neck."

Indeed, this subject is Mr. Alexander's special province and his own experience fully confirms Sherrington's description of the difficulties involved. He says that when he wished to see what he was doing in the act of reciting he derived invaluable help from a mirror. When he set out on an experiment which involved a new use of certain parts of his psycho-physical organism he was under the delusion that "because we are able to do what we 'will to do' in acts that are habitual and involve familiar sensory experiences, we shall be equally successful in doing what we 'will to do' in acts that are contrary to our habit and therefore involve sensory experiences that are unfamiliar." Looking in the mirror, he saw that he was doing the opposite of what he believed he was doing and of what he had decided he ought to do. He also saw that "the use of a specific part

---

*The Universal Constant in Living, 8⁰, London, 1942.

Extract from a letter to Mr. Alexander from Sir Charles Sherrington:—"*I need not repeat to you that I appreciate the value of your teaching and observations. I was glad to take the occasion to say so in print. I know some of the difficulties which attach to putting your ideas across to those less versed in the study than yourself. Your disciples, however, can more and more disseminate them and multiply your call.*"

in any activity is closely associated with the use of other parts of the organism, and that the influence exerted by the various parts one upon another is continuously changing in accordance with the manner of use of these parts. If a part directly employed in the activity is being used in a comparatively new way which is still unfamiliar, the stimulus to use this part in the new way is weak in comparison with the stimulus to use the other parts of the organism, which are being indirectly employed in the activity in the old habitual way." In his own case, he was attempting "to bring about an unfamiliar use of the head and neck for the purpose of reciting. The stimulus to employ the new use of the head and neck was therefore bound to be weak as compared with the stimulus to employ the wrong habitual use of the feet and legs which had become familiar through being cultivated in the act of reciting."

A full account of Alexander's work is given in his four books*; and as he says, "the idea of taking control of the use of the mechanisms of the human creature from the instinctive to the conscious plane has already been justified by the results which have been obtained in practice, but it may be many years before its true significance as a factor in human development is fully recognized."

Mr. Alexander gives personal lessons in his technique at *16, Ashley Place, Westminster, S.W.1.*, with his staff of assistant teachers. Further information may be obtained from his secretary.

*F. MATTHIAS ALEXANDER's books are: *Man's Supreme Inheritance, Constructive Conscious Control of the Individual, The Use of the Self, and The Universal Constant in Living.* All published by Chaterson Ltd. London

Printed & Published by Walter Carrington at the Sheildrake Press, 14, Hadley Gardens, London, W.4. November 1951.

Appendix B: Students of the F. Matthias Alexander Teachers' Training Course 1931–1955.

The year indicates when the students commenced their training. Most teachers qualified after three years. Although the students who started in 1931 qualified after three years they stayed on to do an additional year (with the exception of Marjorie Barstow). The students whose training was interrupted by Alexander's stroke in 1948 also had their training extended. Parenthesis indicates the married name where known. An asterisk (*) indicates that the student did not finish their training. A cross (†) indicates that the student started with F. M. Alexander and finished with A. R. Alexander (in Boston, USA). A double cross (‡) indicates that the student later trained or finished their training with Patrick Macdonald. It has not been possible to verify the accuracy of all the names and dates. The list is compiled primarily from Walter Carrington's copy of the Ashley Place records.

1931	Marjorie Barstow
	Margaret Goldie
	Catharine Merrick*‡ (the Countess Wielopolska)
	George Trevelyan
	Gurney MacInnes
	Jean MacInnes
	Lulie Westfeldt
	Erika Schumann (Whittaker)
1932	Patrick Macdonald
1933	Marjory Mechin (Barlow)
	Charles Neil
1934	Maxwell Alexander
1935	Miss Stallard*
1936	Walter Carrington
	Eric de Peyer
	Margaret Dunlop
	Elizabeth Falkner
	Margaret Lundie*
	Harriet Whitcher*
1937	Alma Frank
	Gertrude Cox*

1947	John Skinner
	Hugo Frischauer*
	Peggy Nixon (Williams)
	John Vicary*
	Mary Lord
	Jim Rawsthorne*
	Bertha E. Baertschi*
1948	Richard Baldock*
	E. Martin*
1949	D. Jones*
	Gordon Chadwick*
	Marion Richardson*
1950	Arthur Ellens*
1951	Anthony Spawforth
1952	Bill Williams
1953	Anna Haddon*
	Goddard Binkley
1954	Stewart Law*
	Constance Tracey*
	Winifred Dussek
1955	Jean Macklin*
	Dorothy Corfe*
	Ted Peacock*
	Pat Peacock*‡
	Dilys Carrington

————— ❧ —————

On the steps of Nº 16 Ashley Place in 1931: Erika Schumann (Whittaker), Margaret Goldie, Jean MacInnes, Marjorie Barstow, Irene Stewart, Gurney MacInnes, (in front) Lulie Westfeldt, Max Alexander, George Trevelyan.

Subject notes

1. Dr Samuel Johnson (1709–84) analysed Hamlet's 'To be or not to be' soliloquy in his edition of *The Plays of William Shakspeare, in 8 vols., with Notes* (1765). Dr Johnson believed that Hamlet is debating the existence of an afterlife before considering the possibility of talking his own life. (Whereas the most common interpretation has been that 'To be or not to be' is a contemplation of suicide.) Hamlet, Dr Johnson writes, 'meditates on his situation in this manner: Before I can form any rational scheme of action under this pressure of redress, it is necessary to decide, whether, *after our present state*, we are *to be or not to be*.' In 1776 Dr Johnson admitted that his interpretation was 'disputable' and his biographer, James Boswell, wrote that his friend Edmond Malone 'has clearly shown [Dr Johnson's interpretation] to be erroneous.' Alexander's remark should be understood in the wider context of Dr Johnson's negative criticisms of the character of Hamlet, and Dr Johnson's dislike of Shakespeare's treatment of Hamlet's 'feigned madness', for which he could see no dramatic purpose and which he found unconvincing.

2. John Keats' poem, *Endymion: A Poetic Romance* (1818) was reviewed in the August 1818 issue of *Blackwood's Edinburgh Magazine*. The insulting and disparaging review was by John Gibson Lockhart who had been hired in order to give *Blackwood's* a more anti-Whig bias. Lockhart – under the pseudonym 'Z' – used Keats' social position and circumstances, and the fact that he had been apprenticed to a surgeon, in order to denigrate his verse. The review ends: 'It is a better and a wiser thing to be a starved apothecary than a starved poet; so back to the shop, Mr John, back to the "plasters, pills, and ointment boxes," &c. But, for Heaven's sake, young Sangrado [doctor], be a little more sparing of extenuatives and soporifics in your practice than you have been in your poetry.' For many years *Blackwood's* continued to refer to Keats as 'Pestleman Jack'. The poem was also brutally attacked in two other journals and Keats was distressed by the criticism.

3. The speech by the Prime Minister, Clement Attlee, which was broadcast on 3rd March 1946, inaugurated a Government campaign for increased production. It followed Attlee's speech (27 February 1946) in the House of Commons in the debate on the problems of reconverting industry to peacetime production. The main problem was the shortage of labour, and the two speeches emphasized the need for people to work harder in order to secure a rapid return to pre-war living standards. The broadcast speech was an appeal for all to serve the country during the difficult time of industrial reconstruction, for the common purpose of prosperity.

4. Aleksei D. Speransky, a Russian researcher of patho-physiology, was the author of *A Basis for the Theory of Medicine* (1935), the result of more than ten years of research. He and his department at the Institute for Experimental Medicine carried out numerous experiments on the rôle of the nervous system in the development of various diseases like rabies, tetanus, dysentery, typhus, measles and others which have a well-defined and fairly uniform, progressive development. The effect of various interferences on the nervous system could then be compared with the expected development of disease. Speransky provides data to show how a seemingly local intervention on the nervous system has effects on the whole nervous system and, in turn, on the animal's 'constitution.' The general conclusion is that the nervous system is not only involved in, but '*organises and determines* many pathological forms which hitherto have been regarded as independent of nervous influence'.

   One of the key experiments was due to the observation that a dog which had fully recovered after it had been given a non-lethal dose of tetanus toxin, nevertheless died of tetanus after undergoing an otherwise harmless operation. Many experiments on cats confirmed that although an organism could survive an initial dose of tetanus, the disease could fully develop if the nervous system was given a different irritant, like an injection of bile, which in itself would not cause any major disease or disturbance to the nervous system. Speransky concluded that if a nerve trauma can 'restore' tetanus at a point where the animal is considered to have recovered from the disease it means that the nervous system has the property of preserving its reaction to the original irritation.

Further experiments showed that the development of tetanus depends on the irritability of the nervous system. For example, when tetanus is introduced into a nerve along with an anaesthetic which inhibits local nervous activity, tetanus does not develop. Likewise, anti-tetanus serum does not exert any curative effect as had previously been thought, but neutralises the irritability caused by the tetanus, thereby preventing the tetanus from spreading through the nervous system. Speransky suggests that old medical methods, like cauterisation by hot iron or cupping glasses, smearing with irritating substances, and subcutaneous injections of protein substances, owed their effect to local interference with the nervous system, i.e. temporary inhibition would diminish the irritability of the nerves and consequently reduce their susceptibility.

The book concludes that it is not yet possible to formulate an all-embracing view of disease and health since it is not known what is 'healthy' or 'normal'. Disease, however, can be characterised by the appearance of a new type of nervous activity: new, but inappropriate reactions which are harmful. Since the reactivity of nerves is not independent of the rest of the nervous system, the consequences of any interference depend upon the 'sum total of all the parts'. Speransky proposes that the operation of the nervous system holds the clues to a unifying theory of medicine.

Since Speransky does not explain how the toxin is prepared, it is not known whether it was the pure tetanus toxin (exotoxin) or the bacillus of tetanus which was used. The latter can probably survive in the organism for a longer period of time.

Alexander knew of Speransky's book: he sent a copy to Dr Mungo Douglas* in 1946.

5. Several ideas – an institute, an association or society, a trust for the preservation and furtherance of the Technique – were considered at this time. One of the proposals was to purchase a mansion in the country which could act as an Alexander Technique centre as well as providing residential quarters for Alexander and other teachers. By bringing all activities and teachers under one roof it was envisaged that it would be possible to run the Little School (previously run at Alexander's residence at Penhill), and the train-

ing course, as well as intensive courses for adults where the Technique could be applied to such activities as horse riding, tennis etc. Sir Stafford* and Dame Isobel Cripps were confident that the money could be raised among Alexander's pupils and other supporters of the Technique. The plans were temporarily shelved, however, because of the South African Libel Case, which did not end until June 1949. Several attempts to set up either a society or a trust floundered for various reasons. Meanwhile Charles Neil,* who taught independently of Alexander and Ashley Place, renamed his teaching centre the Dame Isobel Cripps Centre with her patronage in 1949. Since a major potential financial supporter was no longer in the picture, no further attempts at an institute or trust were pursued.

6. This refers to Alexander's four books, *Man's Supreme Inheritance* (1918), *Constructive Conscious Control of the Individual* (1923), *The Use of the Self* (1932), and *The Universal Constant in Living* (1942). Alexander considered his books especially important for teachers of his Technique: the certificate which the students received upon qualification stated that the teacher was 'qualified to teach the technique outlined in my books'.

7. It was a common superstition that a wart would disappear if it was rubbed with a piece of meat which was then buried and allowed to rot. It is an old belief which was first recorded in Britain in 1579.

8. An 'iron' on the foot or leg refers to a calliper: a surgical brace or metal splint for support.

9. In 1944 an editorial in the South African physical education journal *Manpower* libelled Alexander and his technique. It claimed that Alexander was a quack, dishonest, that he had given the public potentially dangerous and criminally irresponsible advice, that he had for personal gain deliberately distorted and concealed the truth, and that his claim to a scientific basis for his technique was unfounded and nonsensical. When the editors – one of them, Jokl,* had written the article – refused to retract the statements, Alexander sued them for libel for £5,000. Because of the war the case came to court in 1948. Drs Barlow* and Drew* came to South

Africa to given evidence for Alexander who, because of his stroke, was unable to appear. Many of Alexander's pupils testified on his behalf, among them Drs M. Douglas*, P. Macdonald and Sir Stafford Cripps*. The witnesses for the defence were notable scientists (*see* note 29) but as they had no experience of Alexander's work and had read very little of his books, most of their opinions were discarded. As the defence could not prove their claims, e.g. that Alexander's technique did not work and that it wasn't scientific, judgment was given for Alexander in the sum of £1,000. The judgment was appealed but upheld in 1949.

10. The 'bumping' of the heart is not a technical term, so it is not certain what is referred to. Two successive sounds can be heard for each heartbeat in the healthy adult and any deviation from this can indicate various disorders. For example, ejection sounds or 'clicks' are high-pitched sounds caused by the abrupt halting of valve opening; they are often due to high blood pressure (in hypertension, for example).

11. A murmur, caused by turbulent blood flow through the heart, may be harmless but sometimes it can indicate a disease, for example stenosis (narrowing) of the heart valves or some congenital heart disease.

12. As an example of mechanical advantage Alexander describes the procedure of leaning back and resting against a book in *MSI*, p. 115, footnote.

13. When the War ended the government introduced a training scheme for ex-servicemen returning to civil life. Ellen Wilkinson, Minister of Education (1945–47), was in charge of this programme and it was in this connection that Walter Carrington produced a prospectus for the training course (reproduced in facsimile on the endpapers).

14. The lease of Ashley Place was about to expire and it was expensive to renew it. Alexander's attempts to move, first to Carlyle Place and later to Chester Square, however, all failed and in the end he renewed the lease for Ashley Place.

15. Christian Science was founded in the USA in 1879 by Mary Baker Eddy (1821–1910). Her book, *Science and Health with Key to the Scriptures* (1875), is the sourcebook for the study and practice of the Church. One of the key beliefs of the Church is that creation was spiritual: that matter, the source of sin and suffering, is not a God-created substance, but a (false) mode of human perception. Disease or death is therefore a misconception and not a material fact. The only lasting cure is prayer in order to gain 'the mind of Christ,' i.e. a deep understanding of the spiritual order of the world. Despite a relatively small membership (*c.* 269,000 in 1936) Christian Science has aroused considerable controversy; however, the views of its adherents have often been misunderstood.

16. An enlarged and revised edition of *MSI* was published in the USA in January 1918 followed by a (first) reprint in May 1918. However, it was the second reprint which contained appreciations by John Dewey* (one review and two published letters in which he responds to a critical review of *MSI* by Randolph Bourne), Professor Frank Granger,* J. H. Jowett and Professor H. M. Kallen. These appreciations were included in the Methuen edition published in the UK in November 1918 and in all subsequent reprints until 1941 when Chaterson Ltd. (run by F. C. C. Watts*) took over the printing and distribution of Alexander's books. The proposed pamphlet mentioned here was never produced.

17. George Bernard Shaw (1856–1950) collapsed in May 1938 and was diagnosed as suffering from pernicious anaemia. Until shortly before that time the only treatment consisted of eating plenty of raw liver, but this was unacceptable to Shaw, who was a life-long vegetarian and campaigner for the 'Nature Cure.' Instead he employed a new remedy, consisting of 15 monthly injections of liver extract. It was at first successful, but a second collapse in December 1938 made him replace the injections with a herbal remedy called Hepamalt. Although generally frail during the last years of his life, he did not suffer from anaemia again.

18. *Knowing How to Stop* is a 60-page booklet edited by Dr. Wilfred Barlow* and subtitled 'A Technique for the Prevention of the Wrong Use of the Self.' Apart from Dr Barlow's 'Some Objections Answered' it contains previously published articles on the

Technique: 'Instinct and Functioning in Health and Disease' by
Dr Peter Macdonald, 'The F. Matthias Alexander Technique and
its Relation to Education' by I. G. Griffith, 'End-gaining and
Means-Whereby' by Aldous Huxley, 'F. Matthias Alexander and
the Problem of Animal Behaviour' by Dr A. Rugg-Gunn, 'The
Work of F. M. Alexander and the Medical White Paper' by Dr
(Dorothy) Radcliffe Drew*, 'Knowing How to Stop' by Dr Barlow
and 'The F. Matthias Alexander Technique' by Frank P. Jones.
The foreword by F. M. Alexander is taken from *UCL*, being the
chapter 'Knowing How to Stop' which was added to the 1946
edition. Some of these articles were later reprinted in *The Alexander Journal* and *More Talk of Alexander* (edited by Dr Barlow).

19.   The article by E. Jokl* is a much shortened version of the original
44-page editorial in *Manpower* (*see* note 9). The 5-page article in
Journal of Physical Education concentrates its criticism of Alexander
on his claim in *UCL* (p. 116) that Professor Magnus had discovered a 'conscious control mechanism of the individual' and that
Sir Charles Sherrington* had referred to this discovery in a Presidential Address before the Royal Society. Magnus' experiments
were performed on decerebrate animals and so the influence of
the head position relative to the spine is not directly applicable to
conscious human posture. Sherrington did refer to Magnus' discoveries in his address of 1926 but not to a primary control which
is Jokl's interpretation of Alexander. With quotations from the
address Jokl shows that Sherrington did not refer to a conscious
control but, on the contrary, referred to reflex systems which
consciousness cannot 'analyse or control.' Following Alexander's
protest, the Ling Association published a retraction which listed
the article concerned and then read: 'We desire to disassociate the
Ling Physical Education Association and the editorial management of this Journal from the views expressed in the above-
mentioned article and to express to Mr F. M. Alexander our deep
regret for any distress it may have caused him.'
        The Ling Physical Education Association (which existed
until 1954) had previously been named the Ling Association of
Teachers of Swedish Gymnastics.

20.   Rudolf Magnus (1873–1927), German Professor who investigated the physiology of posture, in particular the reflexes of stand-

ing, muscle tone and postural attitude. He proposed the existence of a central control which co-ordinated these reflexes. Alexander referred to Magnus's discovery of a central control both in *UoS* and *UCL*. Magnus's lectures referred to here are 'Animal Posture' (1925), and 'Some Results of Studies in the Physiology of Posture' (1926). (*See also* note 19.)

21. One of the moral defeats which the defendants (Jokl* and the editors of *Manpower – see* note 9) suffered in court was the reduction of security which Alexander was obliged to put up. Under the rules of the court Alexander ranked as *peregrinus* (a foreigner) and could therefore be compelled to give security for the costs of the action, should he lose the case. If the plaintiff failed to pay in advance the required security, the case could not proceed and would automatically be struck off. The defendants made an application for Alexander to give security in the sum of £4,000. This was reduced by the court to £2,000. (It is not known what the second 'moral defeat' was).

22. In 1946 Wilfred and Marjory Barlow* went on holiday to France with Vernon Berrangé* and his wife, Yolande. They invited Alexander to join them. In Paris, when visiting the tomb of Napoleon, Alexander recited one of his favourite poems, which was critical of Napoleon (*see* F. M. Alexander's *Articles and Lectures*). Towards the end of the holiday, in Brittany, while they were temporarily short of money, Alexander attempted at the casino to relieve the shortage but failed: he lost all they had left (*see* M. Barlow's *1965 F. M. Alexander Memorial Lecture.*).

23. Both Duncan Whittaker* and Thomas Pilcher* were psychiatrists. They didn't finish their training in the Technique.

24. *ITMA – It's That Man Again* – was a famous and popular radio comedy programme. It ran on the BBC from 1939 until 1949 when its star, Tommy Handley, died. The title was taken from a reference to Adolf Hitler in a newspaper headline but soon became exclusively identified with Tommy Handley. The acronym was a parody of the wartime outburst of institutions known by their initials and military abbreviations. *ITMA* helped to boost morale through its satire of wartime bureaucracy and by its atti-

tude of 'business as usual'; during the War 16 million people listened to the programme every week. Several of its catch-phrases still exist, e.g. 'I don't mind if I do.'

25. Dr Mungo Douglas'* paper, 'Re-orientation of the View Point upon the Study of Anatomy' attempts to explain the importance of the head-neck relationship in terms of muscular anatomy. It briefly explains the muscles of the neck and their function. It concludes that it is essential to recognise that 'the relationing function of muscle is the primary function of muscle, and that movements of parts upon parts is secondarily,' and that the primary relationing is established by the muscles which comprise the atlas, axis and occipital bones. Alexander quoted an extract from this paper in *UCL*, Appendix C.

26. Arthur J. Busch wrote in *The Brooklyn Citizen* – under the pen-name of Michael March – several articles in support of Alexander and his work. In an article of 7 April 1939 Busch declared that 'Professor Coghill's findings confirm the scientific basis of Alexander's practical work'. Busch also argued that Coghill's* research made 'obsolete practically all of the concepts currently held under the general category of psychology' because they are based on a false premise, i.e. that of separation instead of integration. This point was, however, disputed in a letter by Eric Estorick (1 May). It was in answer to Estorick's criticism that Coghill wrote a letter (12 May) pointing out that his work demonstrated 'a behaviour pattern that was totally integrated from the beginning,' and that having the concept of the organism-as-a-whole and demonstrating it are very different things. Coghill did not comment on Alexander's work. The articles led to an exchange of letters between Coghill and Alexander (who sent Coghill his three books) and later the two men met; Coghill contributed an appreciation to *UCL* in 1941.

27. Both Friedrich Nietzsche (1844–1900) and Richard Wagner (1813–83) were influenced by Arthur Schopenhauer (1788–1860). Alexander is most likely criticizing the reliance on instinct which underlines their philosophies: for example, Nietzsche and Schopenhauer emphasized the importance of Will, which they understood as instinctive; and both of them formulated a theory

of music which proposed that music appealed (and should appeal) to the emotions and the inner dynamism of human life – a theory to which Wagner also subscribed.

Alexander mentions Nietzsche in *MSI* (p. 103) as an illustration of the madness befalling Germany in general.

28. Dr Mungo Douglas'* 'A Unique Example of Operational Verification During Scientific Experimentation' was published in *The Medical Press and Circular* (30 October 1946). Douglas proposes to state the scientific evidence of the Technique: he defines scientific evidence as a 'statement of method or procedure in detail which, when used or followed by anyone, will give rise to means for making further observations', and that the procedure thus constantly verifies itself. Douglas then relates Alexander's development of the Technique (as described in *UoS*) as the perfect example – not of producing facts – but of discovering the means whereby observations may be made. He concludes that Alexander's work is the essence of scientific method.

29. The doctors who gave evidence for the defence in the South African Libel Case (*see* note 9) were Sir A. Webb-Johnson (1880–1958) who was surgeon to H. M. Queen Mary (1936–53) and President of the Royal College of Surgeons; Edgar D. Adrian, Professor of Physiology at Cambridge University and Nobel Prize winner in 1932 (with Sir Charles Sherrington); Sir Henry Dale (1875–1968), President of the Royal Society (1940–45), Doctor of Medicine at Cambridge University and winner of the Nobel Prize in 1936 (with Otto Loewi); Samson Wright (d. 1956) who was Professor of Physiology in the University of London at Middlesex Hospital Medical School (since 1930) and the author of a standard textbook *Applied Physiology* which reached its 9th edition in 1952; Paul H. Wood, Dean at the Institute of Cardiology (1947–50) and author of *Diseases of the Heart and Circulation* (1950); and Freddie Himmelweit who was a director of the Virus Department of the Inoculation Department at St. Mary's Hospital.

30. In the early 1920s F. M. Alexander bought a new car which soon afterwards broke down. He tried to return it to the manufacturers and refused to pay for it. The manufacturers, however, tried to obtain payment and while Alexander was in the USA (he went

there for six months of each year in the period 1918–24), and thus unable to defend himself, they had him declared bankrupt. On his return Alexander applied to the Receiver in Bankruptcy and explained the circumstances of his case. He declared that he would not pay for the car on principle since it did not work and had never worked. The Receiver was sympathetic and said that whereas he could not rescind the bankruptcy order, he could and would relieve Alexander of most of the practical disabilities of it. Alexander was allowed to open and operate a personal bank account and to obtain goods on credit as he wished. Subsequently, friends urged Alexander to apply for his discharge in order to prevent the stigma of bankruptcy from doing damage to Alexander's reputation. Eventually, with Alexander's rather reluctant consent, Dr Peter Macdonald bought the debt for a small sum (from a firm of debt collectors) which cleared the way for an application to be made for a discharge. Unfortunately, the application was mishandled, as it was represented to the Receiver that Alexander had always refused to pay the debt as a matter of principle and that he would sooner die an undischarged bankrupt than pay the debt. The Receiver viewed this as an attitude of unacceptable obstinacy and declared that Alexander should have his wish.

31. Tic douloureux (literally 'painful twitch') is another name for trigeminal neuralgia: a disorder of the trigeminal nerve in which episodes of severe, stabbing pain affect the cheek, lips and gums on one side of the face. The cause is uncertain and treatment is difficult.

      The tic douloureux case referred to here is mentioned in *UCL*, case E in chapter 2 and Appendix E.

32. Raymond Dart's* article, 'The Postural Aspect of Malocclusion' was published in September 1946. The article, 'Voluntary Musculature in the Human Body: The Double–Spiral Arrangement' was scheduled to be published in the *Bulletin of Royal College of Surgeons* in 1946 but was, in fact, not published until 1950, in *The British Journal of Physical Medicine*.

33. Percy Boomer (b. 1884), brother of Aubrey Boomer (b.1897). They were professional British golfers and won several championships in the 1920s. Percy Boomer's *On Learning Golf* (1942)

contains distortions of the concepts and practice of the Alexander Technique.

Boomer expresses his indebtedness to 'Professor' Alexander for demonstrating the psycho-physical unity of all acts in *UoS*. However, concepts are confused when Boomer says that Alexander's conscious control replaces thinking – for Boomer 'thinking' means emotional thoughts. Boomer's description of conscious control is of 'building up *feel*'. In golf this is done, not by thinking, but by 'constant repetition of the correct action', which will build up a 'comfortable and reliable *feel*'. Instead of thinking of where the ball is to go, one should concentrate on the swing by getting the 'feel' of the swing. To be in psycho-physical 'unison' the golfer must feel his swing as '*all one piece*'. One should memorize these muscle sensations. In this way the process of giving the directions 'one after the other' becomes, for Boomer, 'a cycle of sensations'. Boomer recommended that to obtain a good preparatory position for the swing the golfer must 'feel' that the 'hips and shoulders are all braced.' Directing upwards is equivalent, in Boomer's language, to generating an '*upward* brace'. Other concepts of Alexander's featured are 'inhibition', 'end gainer' and 'means whereby', which are just as misleadingly explained.

Biographical notes

'Alexander' or 'F. M.' refers to F. Matthias Alexander; other family members are referred to by their full names. The 'Technique' refers to the F. M. Alexander Technique. An asterisk (*) marks a name that has its own entry.

Alexander, Albert Redden ('AR'), (1873–1947), Australian teacher of the Alexander Technique and F. M.'s younger brother. After service in the Boer War he joined F. M.'s teaching practice in 1901 in Melbourne which he continued after F. M. moved to London in 1904. A. R. joined F. M. in London around 1907–10. In c. 1917 A. R. was paralysed for about six months as the result of a riding accident but recovered, though from then on he walked with a cane and would often sit while teaching the Technique. Between 1915 and 1925 he taught regularly in the USA and in 1933/34 he moved to Boston. He taught on the teachers training course started by F. M., which he continued after F. M. moved to New York towards the end of 1942. Having suffered a stroke in 1944 A. R. returned to England in 1945, where he died.

Alexander, Maxwell (b. 1916), British teacher of the Technique and nephew to F. M. After training with Alexander (1934–37) he taught the Technique with his father, A. R., in Boston. Maxwell Alexander joined the Territorial Army in 1939, rising to the rank of major. He taught the Technique 1946–52 (in the latter years in Nottingham) and then returned to the regular Army. Since 1958 he has been a financial consultant. He gave a lecture on his life with the Technique at the NASTAT AGM in 1992.

Balfour, Arthur James, 1st Earl of Balfour (1848–1930), Scottish statesman and philosopher. In a 50-year-long political career in the Conservative Party he held many influential government posts. As Prime Minister (1902–05) he was responsible for the Anglo-French agreement of 1904 (Entente Cordiale) which signified a major shift in British foreign policy. While serving as Foreign Secretary (1916–19) he made the Balfour Declaration of 1917 which pledged British support for a national homeland for the Zionists in Palestine. He wrote *Defence of Philosophic Doubt* (1879) and gave the 1915 Gifford Lectures, *Theism and Humanism*.

He suffered from delicate health, especially in his youth and following the substantial electoral defeat of 1906. Generally, he would have periods of concentrated effort interspersed with periods of fatigue.

Barlow, Wilfred ('Bill') (1915–91), British doctor and teacher of the Technique. After studying medicine at Oxford Barlow trained with Alexander (1938–45). He worked at Middlesex Hospital (1946–48), specializing in rheumatology. This was discontinued, however, because of his involvement in the South African Libel Case (*see* note 9). He investigated the effects of the Technique on posture and wrote several medical articles on aspects of the Technique, investigating, for example, the relationship between anxiety and muscle tension. He assisted his wife, Marjory, in running a teachers training course (1950–82), while continuing his medical work. He successfully resurrected the plans for a Society of Teachers in 1958. He edited *The Alexander Journal* for many years and published selections from it in *More Talk of Alexander* (1978). Perhaps his best known work is the medically-oriented introduction to the Technique, *The Alexander Principle* (1973).

Barlow, Marjory, *née* Mechin (b. 1915), British teacher of the Technique and niece of Alexander. She trained 1933–36, taught until 1940 at Ashley Place, and was caretaker of Ashley Place while Alexander was in the US (1940–43). She married Wilfred Barlow in 1940 and they ran a teachers training course (1950–82). In 1965 she gave the F. M. Alexander Memorial Lecture, *The Teaching of F. Matthias Alexander*.

Barstow, Marjorie (1899–1995), US teacher of the Technique. After graduating from the University of Nebraska in 1921 she taught ballet and ballroom dancing. In 1927 she went to London and had a six-month course of lessons with F. M. and A. R. Alexander. After her training with Alexander 1931–34, she worked as A. R.'s assistant in Boston. Soon afterwards she had to return to Nebraska to take care of the family business and did not start teaching again until the 1950s. In the 1970s she developed an unconventional approach to the teaching of the Technique by giving brief, individual work in a group setting. Her work is celebrated in *Marjorie Barstow – Her Teaching and Training* (1988, ed. B. Conable).

Berrangé, Vernon C. (1900–83), South African lawyer who acted for Alexander in the Libel Case (*Alexander vs. Jokl, see also* note 9). Berrangé served in the RAF 1918–19, was a successful racing driver in the 1920s and a big game hunter. He was a tireless defender of human rights and was for many years Chairman of the Legal Aid Society. He built up a reputation as an outstanding criminal and political lawyer with a forte for cross-examination. Nelson Mandela relates in his autobiography, *The Long Road to Freedom* (1994), how well Berrangé defended him and 155 other members of the Congress Movement in the Treason Trial 1956–61, on the charge of spreading communist propaganda. (With the help of other defence lawyers all accused were eventually acquitted.) Berrangé had joined the Communist Party in 1938, was 'named' under the Suppression of Communism Act in 1950, and when it appeared that steps might be taken to have him disbarred because he was a listed communist, he arranged for his own name to be removed from the Roll of Advocates and in 1966 exiled himself and his wife, Yolande, to Swaziland where he continued to practise law. Although Berrangé's political views changed and he had ceased to be a communist by the early 1960s, he refused to publicly repudiate or criticize his former comrades.

Yolande, who had lessons with Irene Tasker, was the connecting link between Berrangé and Alexander.

Best, Robert Dudley (1892–1984), British businessman. Best inherited his family brass foundry, Best & Lloyd, known for their lamps (in 1893 they invented the 'Surprise' pendant which was the forerunner of today's angle-poise lamp). In World War I Best served as an Observer in the Royal Flying Corps. As a result of being wounded in action he began to suffer from neck spasms; he started having lessons in 1929 and became a keen supporter of the Technique. He encouraged teachers to practise in Birmingham and Patrick Macdonald,* Erika Whittaker,* Irene Stewart* and Anthony Spawforth taught at his home in Edgbaston. Best's son, John, went to Alexander's Little School at Penhill. In the 1940s Robert Best worked on an unfinished essay, 'Conscious Constructive Criticism,' in which he criticizes dogmatic approaches to the teaching of the Technique.

Caldwell, John Revie (1892–1967), British doctor and radiologist. He qualified in 1914 and became a captain in the Royal Army Medical Corps. He also served in the British Expeditionary Force. He was one of 19 doctors who signed a letter to *BMJ* (29 May 1937; quoted in *UCL*) calling for an official investigation into the Technique so that it could be recognized by the medical establishment. He had a private practice in Milnthorpe, Westmorland.

Campbell, Brian (b. 1921), South African teacher of the Technique. He was accepted on Alexander's teachers training course at the unusual age of 17, provided he did an extra year of training. He trained 1938–40 (for which his father paid) and 1946–48, serving in the South African Army during the war. Unable to teach full-time following his return to South Africa in 1947, he became a businessman and market researcher. After a refresher course for teachers he took up full-time teaching in 1965 until his retirement in 1991.

Carrington, Dilys M. G. (b. 1915), British teacher of the Alexander Technique. After gaining a B.Sc. in mathematics and psychology she worked as a secretary. In 1940 Dilys and Walter married. They have three children: Christopher (b. 1941), Richard (b. 1943) and Matthew (b. 1947). She trained as a teacher 1955–60 and has since 1960 been co-director with Walter of their teacher training course, The Constructive Teaching Centre Ltd.

Coghill, George Ellett (1872–1941), US professor of anatomy and researcher into the development of reflexes of movement in vertebrates. He worked at several universities and it was during his teaching at the University of Kansas (1913–25) that he carried out a large-scale study of the embryonic behaviour of the American newt, amblystoma. In 1925 he became a full-time researcher at the Wistar Institute of Anatomy and Biology, and in subsequent years he won increasing recognition for his work through his many lecture tours. He provided a comprehensive overview of his work in three lectures delivered in 1928 at the University of London, *Anatomy and the Problem of Behaviour*. Throughout his life

Biographical notes

he was also associated with the *Journal of Comparative Neurology*, as contributor, editor and assistant editor.

The director of the Wistar Institute was not successful in his management, and strained relations developed between him and the staff. Coghill clashed with the director many times when the latter, on financial grounds, refused Coghill essential equipment. In spite of these adverse conditions Coghill was successful in continuing his research. In 1935 his work was abruptly terminated when he was dismissed from the Institute without warning, given no other reason than that his work had been sponsored by an individual who had discontinued the funding. Some of his papers were dumped outside his house and he was refused access to other papers, although these were later provided on loan.

After this forced retirement he continued his work in his home in Gainesville, Florida, supported by the Josiah Macy, Jr., Foundation. Recurrent cardiac attacks and partial paralysis made work increasingly difficult, though, and he died at home of a heart attack on 23 July 1941.

Cripps, Sir (Richard) Stafford (1889–1952), British politician. A lawyer, Cripps entered Parliament in 1931 as a left-wing Labour MP, antiwar and pro-Soviet. He served as Ambassador to Moscow (1940–42) and later served in Winston Churchill's wartime cabinet. As Chancellor of the Exchequer (1947–5), he presided over the post-war austerity program. Cripps and his wife, Dame Isobel, started having lessons with Alexander in 1937 or 1938. In 1949 Dame Isobel became the patron of the Dame Isobel Cripps Centre (formerly The Re-Education Centre), in Holland Park, which was run by one of Alexander's teachers, Charles Neil*, until 1959.

Dailey, Philomene ('Dolly'), US teacher of the Technique. She trained 1942–45 with A. R. Alexander. After her training she took over a demonstration class set up by Margaret Goldie at the Quaker school, Media Friends School, Philadelphia. Without the prior knowledge of F. M. or A. R. Alexander, she started, or attempted to start, her own teachers training programme in the Technique. It is assumed that it was not successful.

Dart, Raymond Arthur (1893–1988), Australian-born South African anatomist and anthropologist. He graduated in medicine at Syd-

ney in 1917, worked with Grafton Elliot Smith in London and
became Professor of Anatomy at Witwatersrand University, Johannesburg, in 1923. He achieved international fame as an anthropologist with his discovery of a branch of the human family,
Australopithecus africanus, in 1925. Having lessons in the Technique with Irene Tasker* in 1943 led Dart to the study of the
embryological and neurological origin of the erect posture and
the importance of poise for learning. Significant articles in this
respect are 'The Postural Aspect of Malocclusion' (1946), 'The
Attainment of Poise' (1947) and 'Voluntary Musculature of the
Human Body: The Double–Spiral Arrangement' (1950). In 1970
he gave the F. M. Alexander Memorial Lecture, 'An Anatomist's
Tribute to F. Matthias Alexander.' He continued to write and
lecture after his retirement in 1958 and was involved with the
Institutes for the Achievement of Human Potential, in Philadelphia.

Dawson of Penn, Viscount B. E. (1864–1945), British Physician to the
King and prominent member of the British Medical Association.
He was involved in setting up the Ministry of Health and as early
as 1918 argued for the creation of a National Health Service.
Although he had served as President of the BMA in 1932 he was
elected again in 1943 and 1944 in order to oversee the setting up
of the National Health Service.

de Peyer, Eric (1906–90), British teacher of the Technique. After graduating in English from Oxford he studied archaeology for a short
time before joining Alexander's training course (1936–39). He
worked with Charles Neil* at The Re-Education Centre (of
which de Peyer was vice-principal) until 1953 when he set up his
own practice in Chelsea. From 1979 he also practised in West
Wittering until increasing incapacity from Parkinson's Disease
forced him to retire. He wrote several introductory articles on the
Technique.

Dewey, John (1859–1952), US philosopher, best known for his philosophy of education and pragmatism. Dewey and Alexander met
in New York in 1916 and began a life-long friendship. Dewey
wrote the introductions to the revised edition of *MSI* (1918), to
CCC (1923) and to *UoS* (1932). Dewey contributed 'invaluable

suggestions' to the manuscript for *CCC* (as Alexander states in his preface).

Donat, (Frederick) Robert (1905–58), English actor. From 1930 he acted in London's West End where he also worked briefly as a manager. He is known for leading rôles in the films *The Thirty-Nine Steps* (1935), *Goodbye Mr Chips* (1939) and *The Citadel* (1938); in the last he played an idealistic doctor who comes to Harley Street from a mining village in Wales. Donat's health was delicate all his life and and he suffered from occasional depressions. 1946 was a particularly difficult year: he had recurring asthmatic attacks, he divorced and his two theatre productions were not successful, losing him £12,000.

Douglas, Dr Mungo, Scottish doctor. He became a doctor in 1921 and practised in Bolton most of his life. He was a pupil and friend of Alexander and wrote several letters to medical journals in support of the Technique as well as some articles, e.g: 'Re-Orientation of the View Point upon the Study of Anatomy' (1937, *see* note 25) and 'A Unique Example of Operational Verification During Scientific Experimentation' (1946, *see* note 28).

Frank, Alma (1898–1953), US teacher who trained 1937–40 and taught until her death in New York City. Her article 'A Study in Infant Development' in *Child Development* (March 1938) examined the links between infant development and the discoveries of Alexander, Magnus and Coghill. Her daughter, Deborah Caplan, also became a teacher of the Technique.

Granger, Frank Stephen (1864–1936), British Professor of Classics and Philosophy. He was Professor at the University of Nottingham (1893–1935), and translated a number of classical texts as well as writing several books, among them *The Worship of the Romans* (1895), *Psychology* (1891) and *Historical Sociology* (1911). His appreciation of *MSI* was published in the book in 1918 and in subsequent reprints but excluded, presumably by mistake, from the 1942 and 1946 editions by Chaterson. In it he writes, 'I have been much impressed by what seems to me a most valuable contribution to psychology. . .' and, 'Mr Alexander has accumulated a large store of experience, and he seems to me to be singularly successful in giving a clear expression to the important results which have disclosed themselves to him.'

Gray, Marjorie ('Chile'), (b. 1915), British teacher of the Alexander Technique. She trained as a Montessori teacher 1932–34. After a series of lessons with Marjory Barlow* she trained with Alexander 1946–48. Gray worked as a school teacher as well as teaching the Technique (which she continues to do). She married Geoffrey Eagar in 1950 and they moved to Wales in 1974.

Haynes, Edmund Sidney Pollock (1877–1949), solicitor and author. Haynes was a keen campaigner for a reform of the divorce laws which he argued for in several articles and books (on the 'anomalies of the marriage laws' as he put it). He also wrote several works on the importance of individual liberty, political and religious, especially warning against increasing bureaucracy. Principally an essayist, his best known works are *A Lawyer's Notebook* (1932) and its sequels, consisting of maxims, profiles and general observations on diverse subjects. Walter Carrington met Haynes when he invited Haynes for the annual dinner of the Chesterton Society at St. Paul's School, and they became lifelong friends.

Hellstenius, Lydia S. ('Lili'), (1903–94), Norwegian student of the Technique. She started her training in 1938 but returned to Norway in 1939 because of the War. Her two children, Erik and Jan, attended classes at the Little School at Penhill. She did some extra training in 1950 or 51 but could not continue and took up the work of J. G. Bennett.

Holland, Sidney (1908–89), British business manager and teacher of the Technique. Inspired by Aldous Huxley's reference to the Technique in *Eyeless in Gaza*, Holland started having lessons in 1939. He trained 1945–49 (an extra year was required because of Alexander's stroke) although he didn't start full-time teaching until 1974 when he had retired as the London manager of Avery Scales. (He applied the principles of the Technique so successfully to his work that the employees rejected having a union because, they said, he looked after them better than a union would.)

Biographical notes

Irving, Sir Henry (1838–1905), English actor-manager. It was in Shake-spearean roles that he gained his reputation as the greatest English actor of his time. He became the first actor to receive a knighthood. Of his sons, Henry Brodribb was also an actor and a pupil of Alexander.

Jokl, Ernst (b. 1907), German-born doctor. Jokl was a talented athlete and twice won national championships. In 1933 he emigrated to South Africa where he specialized in sports medicine. He was head of the department for physical education at Witwatersrand Technical College (from 1938) and medical consultant to the Army (1940–45). After the war he became Director of Medical Research of the National Advisory Council of Physical Education (1945–50). In 1953 he became Director of the Exercise Research Laboratories at the University of Kentucky. He worked with several associations and bodies relating to physical fitness: for example, he was President of the Research Committee of UNESCO's Council of Sport and Physical Education (1956–78?). He wrote several books and articles on the physiology of exercise and sports medicine as well as two autobiographies, and he was a member of the editorial staff of the *Journal of Sports Medicine* and the *American Corrective Therapy Journal*.

Jokl was co-editor of the South African Journal for Physical Education, *Manpower*, and wrote the long editorial, 'Quackery versus Physical Education' (March 1944) which libelled Alexander (*see* note 9).

Lane, Dr W. Arbuthnot (1856–1943), Scottish surgeon. He was Senior Surgeon at Guy's Hospital and Great Ormond St. Hospital and made major contributions to the surgical treatment of bone fractures and chronic constipation.

Lee, Gerald Stanley (1862–1944), US ordained minister of the Congregational Church, and author. He wrote popular books on religious subjects and was a Lecturer on Literature and the Arts at Smith College. He and his wife had lessons from Alexander in 1919 and Lee paid generous tribute to Alexander and the Technique in his book, *The Ghost in the White House* (1920). He subsequently plagiarized Alexander's technique in his *Invisible Exercise* (1922), claiming the discovery of a 'single control' and other main features of the Technique for himself. Alexander's technique was further watered down in Lee's next book, *Rest Working* (1925?) which emphasizes relaxation and the 'balancing' of the workings of one's glands for health and well-being.

Lucas, Edward Verrall (1868–1938), author and chairman of Methuen & Co. publishers. Among his writings are two autobiographies, eleven fictional works, twelve art and travel companions, twelve anthologies of essays and miscellaneous works. He also edited the first complete edition of the letters of Charles and Mary Lamb.

Macdonald, Patrick ('Pat'), (1910–91), British teacher of the Technique. His father, Dr Peter Macdonald, was a friend and supporter of Alexander, and he brought Patrick for lessons with Alexander, beginning in 1920. Patrick joined the first training course in 1931, qualifying in 1935, and he worked as an assistant at Ashley Place until 1949, serving in the RAF during the war. He worked in Birmingham and Cardiff but moved to Brighton in 1953 and settled in Lewes in 1961. He ran a teachers training course in London (1957–87) as well as an individual practice. His draft for a book was published as *The Alexander Technique As I See It* (1989).

McDonagh, James E. R. (1881–1965), English surgeon, Alexander's doctor and friend. McDonagh first had lessons in 1925. He was founder and director of the Nature of Disease Institute from 1929 in which he researched the underlying factors common to different kinds of diseases. His *The Nature of Disease* (3 vols.,1924–27-31) (as well as its follow-up studies) is based on the concept that 'there is only one disease', and that what is known as disease is merely a manifestation of damage suffered by protein in the blood. Health depends on the harmonious threefold activity of protein which he proposes to be 'radiation, attraction and storage'. In his books he attempted to develop a unitary theory of medicine. He makes references to Alexander's technique in several of his works.

MacInnes, Gurney, British teacher of the Technique. He came into contact with Alexander in 1927 through A. G. Pite who shortly afterwards became Headmaster of Weymouth College, a boys' preparatory school. MacInnes taught at the Junior School at Weymouth for two terms before joining Alexander's training course (1931–34). Pite was anxious to introduce the Technique into the school and MacInnes worked in Weymouth College, giving both individual lessons and working with individuals during various activities (1936–39). After serving in the Army during the War, MacInnes took up farming and did not teach the Technique again.

Morrison, Dr Dorothy S. R., *née* Drew (1908–88), British surgeon and gynaecologist. She gained her MD in 1935 and was later awarded a Gold Medal in Gynaecology. She first started having lessons in 1943, suffering from sinusitis, appendix trouble, irregular heart rhythm, fatigue from overwork and from injuries sustained in a car accident several years before. The Technique was successful in curing or relieving many of these conditions, a fact to which she testified in the South African Libel Case (*see* note 9); on that occasion she also provided fifteen impressive case studies of the beneficial effects of the Technique out of the 150 cases which she had collected. She started training with Alexander in 1946 but did not teach the Technique; she studied acupuncture and continued working as a GP. Her approach to illness, however, was from then on informed by her knowledge of the Technique, acupuncture and massage. She moved to South Africa in 1956 where she continued her private medical practice as well as lecturing in several countries on acupuncture.

Murdoch, Dr Andrew (1863–1943), British doctor. After graduating in 1884 he settled in Bexhill-on-Sea where he built up a large private practice. He was an active member of the BMA. He wrote several letters to the *BMJ* in support of Alexander's work and published a booklet, 'The Function of the Sub-Occipital Muscles – The Key to Posture, Use and Functioning'. He wrote an unfinished paper on the Technique, 'Basic Physical Culture and Physical Training'.

Murray, Alan (1897–1975), Australian teacher of the Technique. He studied acting and music and joined a theatre company. In the early 1920s, after a tour of the USA, he settled in New York, teaching, acting and producing plays. Later he became interested in Alice Bailey's work and joined her Arcane School of Philosophy and Comparative Religion. He taught first at her centre in New

York, and from 1937 at her centre in Kent, England. Alan Murray trained with Alexander 1946–50 and returned to Australia upon completion. He first lived and taught in Melbourne and, from 1954, in Sydney.

Neil, Charles Alexander (1916–58), British teacher of the Technique. Neil suffered from severe asthmatic attacks which the Technique alleviated to a great extent. He trained 1933–36 and left Ashley Place in 1937 to teach on his own. After the war, in which he served in India, he set up the Re-Education Centre in Holland Park (*c.* 1947), which became the Dame Isobel Cripps Centre in 1949 when Dame Isobel Cripps became a patron of the centre. Neil taught his own postural relaxation method – an offshoot of the Technique – which he described in the Family Doctor Booklet 'Poise and Relaxation' (*c.* 1958).

Nichols, Robert M. B. (1898–1944), English poet. After serving in the RAF during World War I he became Professor of English Literature at Tokyo University (1921–24). He published several collections of poems as well as plays, romances and a novella.

Pilcher, Thomas D. (1908–67), British psychiatrist. He became a surgeon in 1937 and was Medical Officer in the Navy during World War II. After the war he was Honorary Physician at Bethlem Royal Hospital of Mental and Nervous Disease. He was also a keen watercolour painter. He joined Alexander's training course in 1946 but did not finish the training. He retired in 1950.

Pirow, Oswald (1890–1959), South African politician and lawyer. He was educated in Germany and then read law in London, winning the Inner Temple Scholarship for Jurisprudence. During this time he excelled as a sportsman, becoming English champion javelin thrower and reaching international standard in several other disciplines. In 1914 he started practising law in Pretoria, gaining a reputation for a being an astute cross-examiner. He entered politics as a supporter of the National Party, and became an MP in 1924; he was for many years a Minister (of Justice in 1929, of Railways and Harbours, and Defence in 1933, of Trade and Commerce 1938-39). In 1933 he visited Adolf Hitler, and his subsequent sympathy with Germany showed itself first in his unpopular proposal in 1936 that all German possessions in Africa, including South West Africa, should be returned to Germany, and secondly, when World War II broke out, in his support of a neutrality motion. In 1940 Pirow founded his own party, which rejected 'British–Jewish imperialism' and capitalism, as well as the principles of democracy, in order to create a 'White, Christian National Socialist republic'. The New Order party gained 16 seats in 1942 but disappeared after the war. In 1957 he retired from the Law, but returned at government request to lead the state advocates in an important high treason case.

Pirow was one of the defence lawyers for the editors of *Manpower* in the *Alexander v. Jokl and others* Libel Case of 1948–49 (*see* note 9).

Price, Charles, golfer and writer on golf. He won several amateur and open golf tournaments in the USA. He edited the magazine *Golf* and wrote numerous articles on golf. He wrote *The World of Golf* (1963) and edited *Pro Pointers and Stroke Savers* (1960).

Price-Williams, Douglass R. (b. 1924), British-born US Emeritus Professor of Psychiatry and Anthropology. He served in the Merchant Navy 1943–45 and was called up in 1946 for the Armed Services. He was training with Alexander at this time (1945–48) and Alexander and Sir Stafford Cripps appealed on Price-Williams' behalf. Although these appeals were officially rejected he received a cancellation notice three days before he was scheduled to join and he was not called up again. Price-Williams taught in Copenhagen and London (1948–54) after which he became a lecturer in psychology. In 1964 he moved to the US where he became Professor of Psychology at Rice University, Texas. Between 1971 and 1992 he was Professor of Psychiatry and Anthropology at the University of California. He has written numerous papers on psychology, psychiatry and anthropology; his work as an anthropologist has included several cross-cultural field studies. He wrote 'The Relaxation of Muscle Tension' for *The Alexander Journal* (1966) and gave the closing address at the first three International Congresses of the Alexander Technique (1986, 1988, 1991).

Robinson, James Harvey (1863–1936), US historian specializing in European History, about which he wrote several works. He was Professor of History at Columbia University 1895–1919 and a founding member of the New School for Social Research in New York where he lectured (1919–21). He met Alexander in New York in 1916 and wrote a review in praise of *MSI* entitled 'The Philosopher's Stone' in the Atlantic Monthly (April 1919). His best known work is *The Mind in the Making* (1921) which argues for the necessity of free thought if civilization is to progress.

Rowntree, Joseph (1836-1925), businessman, philanthropist and pupil of Alexander; director of the family company of the same name trading in cocoa and confectionery. He hired Dr Peter Macdonald (who went on to have lessons with Alexander) as company doctor. Alexander quotes Rowntree in *UoS* and in *UCL*.

Sandow, Eugene, *née* Friedrich W. Müller (1867–1925), German-born 'strongman' and physical culture teacher; regarded as the founder of modern body-building. Although the history of Sandow's youth is obscure, it seems fairly certain that he visited the then popular German gymnasiums (Jahn's *Turnhalle*) from his early teens onwards. At the age of 17 or 18 he joined a travelling circus where he had some success as an acrobat. In Brussels he met another successful strongman, Attila, who gave Sandow the progressive weight training needed to develop his muscles to their fullest. Sandow performed strongman shows and also worked as a model in Belgium, Holland, France and Italy. His career in England was launched in 1889 by Attila who invited him to take up the challenge of two strongmen performing in London, Sampson and Cyclops. Like many strongmen of the period Sampson and Cyclops would announce a prize, in this case £500, to anyone who could duplicate their feats. Many of their feats, however, were based more on trickery and dexterity than pure strength but, with Attila's help, Sandow outperformed them. (Although Sandow could lift a horse carrying a man – and more – it was not done on this occasion.) Sandow settled in London where he became the foremost physical culture teacher between the late 1890s and World War I. He ran several gymnasia, and sold equipment as well as books and magazines on his physical culture system. Alexander would probably first have heard of him during Sandow's much publicised tour of Australia and New Zealand in 1903.

Alexander later referred to Sandow as an example of the inaccurate method of taking chest size as an indication of lung volume (vital capacity) in his booklet, *The Theory and Practice of a New Method of Respiratory Re-Education* (1907), included in the revised edition of *MSI* (1918).

Sherrington, Sir Charles S. (1857–1952), English neurophysiologist and Nobel Prize winner. By introducing fundamental terms and concepts he laid the foundations for modern neuroscience. His best known works are *The Integrative Action of the Nervous System* (1906) and *Man on His Nature* (1940) – Alexander quotes from the latter in *UCL*. Although Sherrington did not have lessons he acknowledged the importance of Alexander's work in his biography, *The Endeavour of Jean Fernel* (1946), stating that 'Mr Alexander has done a service to the subject [of correcting bad habits of movement] by insistently treating each act as involving the whole integrated individual, the whole psycho-physical man. To take a step is an affair, not of this or that limb solely, but of the total neuro-muscular activity of the moment – not least of the head and neck.' (*See also* APPENDIX A, p. 67.)

Skinner, John (1912–92), British teacher of the Technique. Skinner served in the Royal Australian Air Force, and was a POW under the Japanese. He had read of Alexander's work in Aldous Huxley's *Ends and Means* and wrote immediately after the war to Alexander who responded encouragingly. Skinner arrived in London in November 1946, started training in January 1947 and soon afterwards took over the job of secretary from Walter Carrington. He was secretary and administrator and gave great support to Alexander during difficult times: the South African Trial and Alexander's stroke. After Alexander's death in 1955 he remained secretary of the training course which was continued by Walter Carrington, Margaret Goldie, Irene Stewart and Peggy Williams. When the training course moved to Holland Park in 1962 he carried on his individual teaching practice, sharing premises with Margaret Goldie, in Soho Square.

Spicer, Dr Robert Henry Scanes (1856–1925), a leading throat specialist who became an enthusiastic pupil and supporter of Alexander's
technique upon Alexander's arrival in London in 1904. They fell
out around 1909, however, when Spicer in various lectures and
published letters attempted to claim Alexander's discoveries for
himself. Alexander defended himself against Spicer in the articles
'Why We Breathe Incorrectly' (1909) and 'A Protest Against
Certain Assumptions' (1910).

Stewart, (Janet) Irene (1906–1990), Scottish teacher of the Technique.
Irene was a District Commissioner of the Girl Guide Movement
but, suffering from asthma, she moved to London after hearing
about the Technique from Margaret Goldie. She trained 1931–
34 and subsequently taught at Ashley Place. Together with Alexander, Ethel Webb, Margaret Goldie and the Little School she
went to USA in 1940, returning in 1943. As one of Alexander's
assistants and friends she often drove him places, went riding with
him and joined him for weekends at Penhill. She was also for
many years an active member of the London Scottish Country
Dance Society. In 1963 she retired to live in Carrbridge,
Invernesshire, where she taught only occasionally.

Tasker, Irene (1887–1977), British teacher of the Technique. She was
employed by the Montessori Society who sent her to Rome to
study under Maria Montessori and to translate Montessori's books
into English. It was in Rome that she met Ethel Webb and first
read Alexander. She started having lessons with Alexander in
1913 and became one of Alexander's assistants in 1917. In 1924
she started a school for children, run on the principles of the
Technique, at Ashley Place. It was later transferred to Alexander's
estate at Penhill. Between 1935 and 1949 she taught in South
Africa, where she published an article on the Technique in the
South African Journal of Science. Upon her return she taught in
Cambridge and London and later in Hove.

Thomas, Edith, British teacher of English, which she taught according
to the Berlitz method. She lived in Hungary for a long time before
returning to England in *c.* 1949 when she stayed with the
Carringtons for three years. She had taught English to goverment
ministers, doctors and other prominent people – one of them was

Father Bologh, a Jesuit Priest, who helped Walter Carrington to escape from a POW hospital in Hungary.

Vicary, John Graham. John Vicary's mother was the estatekeeper of Alexander's Penhill House, Kent. John Vicary joined Alexander's training course for a short time in 1947 before he moved to Lundy Island, in the Bristol Channel. An injury, however, obliged him to move to a less isolated place and he settled in Bideford, Devon.

Walker, Elisabeth (b. 1914), British radiographer and teacher of the Technique. In 1935 she worked as assistant to a leading radiologist in London and later at King's College Hospital. She started training with Alexander in 1938 and qualified in 1947. She moved in 1948 to South Africa but returned in 1961, working, among other places, at the New College of Speech and Drama. In 1971 she moved to Oxfordshire where she started a teachers training course in 1984 with her husband.

Walker, Richard Sutherland ('Dick'), (1911–92), British teacher of the Technique. Walker was a successful amateur golfer in Scotland who read *UoS* and started having lessons with the purpose of improving his golf. He started training in 1938, but it was interrupted by the War. During the War he was a Lieutenant in the Navy (RNVR), and served in the Mediterranean. Upon qualifying in 1946 he worked at Ashley Place and in 1949 moved to South Africa to set up practice and replace Irene Tasker who was returning to London. In 1961 he and his wife moved to London, and he worked on the training course run by Dr and Mrs Barlow as well as at the New College of Speech and Drama. He was chairman of STAT in 1970 and delivered the F. M. Alexander Memorial Lecture in 1971. In 1971 he and his wife moved to Oxfordshire where they started a training course in 1984.

Waterston, David (1872–1942), Scottish surgeon. He graduated (MD) with gold medal in 1900. For twelve years he was Demonstrator of Anatomy at Edinburgh University and in 1909–14 Professor of Anatomy at King's College, London, a post which he resigned to become Professor of Anatomy at St. Andrews (1914–42). He researched the mechanism of pain and was author and illustrator of *Anatomy in the Living Model* (1931); he published several papers on anthropology, embryology and comparative anatomy. A friend of Sir James Mackenzie, he became an honorary consultant to the James Mackenzie Institute for Clinical Research upon Sir James' death.

Watts, Frederick C. Chatto (1896–1953), British publisher. He was son of the founder of the Rationalist Press Association, of which he was managing director and chairman. He succeeded his father as editor of the *Literary Guide and Rationalist Review*. He was chairman of C. A. Watts & Co. and originator of the very successful series 'Thinker's Library'. Watts created the imprint 'Chaterson' for Alexander's books, taking over the publication of the books from Methuen in 1941.

Westfeldt, Lulie (1898–1965), US teacher of the Technique. At the age of seven she had poliomyelitis, the scars of which caused her some disability. On the advice of a friend she went in 1929 to London where she had lessons with Alexander. She joined the first teachers training course in February 1931, qualifying in 1935. She taught in New York from 1937 until her death. Her experiences of training and teaching are related in her book, *F. Matthias Alexander – The Man and His Work* (1964).

Webb, Ethel Mary ('Pip'), (1866–1952), teacher of the Technique and assistant to Alexander. It was after reading Alexander's first book in 1910 that she started having lessons. She soon became one of Alexander's most valued assistants, working as secretary, administrator and teacher. She retired as secretary after World War II but continued to look after some of the administration until her death.

Whittaker, Duncan (1906–68), English psychiatrist and pupil of Alexander. He was Senior Assistant Physician at the Bethlem Royal Hospital, a mental hospital, and married Erika in 1940. He first heard of Alexander in Aldous Huxley's *Ends and Means* in 1938 and afterwards read *CCC* before having lessons. In September 1946 he joined the training course for a brief period.

Whittaker, Erika, *née* Schumann (b. 1911), German-born British teacher of the Technique. She started having lessons at the age of eight from her aunt, Ethel Webb. She trained with Alexander 1931–34 and taught the Technique briefly in London and Birmingham. After her marriage to Duncan she lived near Croydon and only occasionally visited Ashley Place. She had one daughter, Anne, in 1943. Erika suffered from TB at the end of the war but rejected medical treatment, and the TB subsided by itself. In 1963 she went to live in Melbourne. She worked in New Guinea for three years and later studied Arabic and Comparative Religion of the Ancient Middle East at Melbourne University. She began teaching the Technique again in 1984.

Wilson, Woodrow (1856–1924), US President 1913–21. Wilson studied political law and became Professor of Jurisprudence and Political Economy at Princeton University where he taught 1890–1910. He wrote *A History of the American People* (1902) and other works. He was also President of the University (1902–10) until he became Governor of New Jersey (1910–13). As American President he is remembered for his 'high-minded and sometimes inflexible idealism' (*Encyclopædia Britannica*). He was a leading advocate of the League of Nations and he opposed, and avoided, US participation in World War I until 1917. He received the 1919 Nobel Peace Prize.

Wint, Guy (1910–1969), British journalist, civil servant and writer. He worked for the League of Nations (1932–36), for the Government of India (1940–46) and for the *Manchester Guardian*. From 1957 he was affiliated to St. Anthony's College, Oxford University. He published several works on Middle Eastern and Asian contemporary politics and conflicts. He also wrote (with Calvocoressi) *Total War: Causes and Courses of the Second World War* (1972). Wint had lessons with Alexander and following Alexander's death he continued lessons with Walter Carrington.

Index

Page numbers in roman refer to the diary. Page numbers in italics refer to the notes; a page number in bold italics refers to a main endnote entry on the subject.

Index

Index

Lee, Gerald S. 30, **95**
Lee, Mr 26
legs 6, 13, 38
Leishman, Dr 58, 59, 64
Libel Case (South African) 8, 26, 47,
   78–79, *88*, 89, *97*, 99, *101*
Lindwall 52
Ling Association 40, 42, 43, 44, 55, *81*
Little School 47, 77, 89, *94*, *102*
Lloyd George, David, 1st Earl of
   Dwyfor 51
Lockhart, J. G. 75
Long Road to Freedom (Mandela) *89*
Lord, Mary 29, 43
Lucas, Edward Verrall 16, *96*
Lytton, Lord 23

Macdonald, Alice 57
Macdonald, Dr Peter 79, *81*, *96*, *100*
Macdonald, Mrs. 48
Macdonald, Patrick 1, 2, 4, 6, 8, 10,
   11, 12, 14, 17, 18, 19, 20, 22, 23, 25,
   27, 29, 30, 34, 35, 36, 37, 38, 39, 40,
   41, 42, 43, 44, 45, 46, 48, 50, 51, 52,
   53, 54, 55, 56, 57, 59, 60, 61, 63, 64,
   89, **96**
MacInnes, Gurney **96–97**
MacInnes, Jean 23, 36
Mackenzie, Sir James *104*
Macy Foundation. *See* Josiah Macy, Jr.,
   Foundation
Madeleine 56
Magnus, Rudolf *81*, *93*
malocclusion 61
Malone, Edmond 75
Man on His Nature (Sherrington) *101*
Manchester Guardian 55
Mandela, Nelson *89*
Manpower *78*, *81*, *82*, *95*, *99*
Man's Supreme Inheritance (Alexander)
   26, 48, 62, *78*, *79*, *80*, *84*, *92*, *93*, *100*,
   101
March, Michael (pen name). *See*
   Busch, Arthur J.
Margot 52
*Marjorie Barstow, Her Teaching and
   Training* (ed. Conable) *89*

Marshall 54
McDonagh, J. E. R. 4, **96**
means-whereby 6, 7, 9, 12, 13, 17, 63
Medical Press and Circular 57
Methuen & Co. 61, *96*, *104*
Meyers 32
Mills 44, 45
Milson, Ronnie 37, 46, 48
Mind in the Making (Robinson) *100*
Ministry of Labour 16
Mitchell, Mrs 64
Montessori, Maria *102*
More Talk of Alexander (ed. Barlow) *81*,
   88
Morgan, Mr 28
Morrison, David 19, 52, 60
Morrison, Dr Dorothy. *See* Drew.
Morrison, Hamish 48
Morrison, Mr (Dorothy's father) 48,
   53
Mount Bischoff Tin-Mining Company
   65, 66
Müller, Friedrich W.. *See* Sandow,
   Eugene
Murdoch, Dr Andrew 15, 58, **97**
Murray, Alan 34, **97–98**
Murray, John 63

Nature of Disease (McDonagh) *96*
neck 8, 46, 53, 59
Neil, Charles 15, 17, 45, 47, 56, *78*, 91,
   92, **98**
Nichols, Robert **98**
Nietzsche, Friedrich 51, *83*
Norris, Jack 5, 10, 18

On Learning Golf (Boomer) 63, **85–86**

Pathfinder Association/Club 27, 28,
   34, 56, 63
Pavlov, Ian 58
Peacy, Belinda 54
Pedley, Eric 60
Penhill 48, 50, 77, *89*, *94*, *102*, *103*
pernicious anaemia 31

The full Fee for the Training Course is Five Hundred Pounds; and this amount has to be paid as follows;-

£125 on entering the Course.

£100 at the beginning of the Third Session.

£75   at the beginning of the Fifth Session.

£75 at the beginning of the Second Session.

£75 at the beginning of the Fourth Session.

£50 at the beginning of the Sixth Session.

Before they enter the Training Course, all Students are required to sign an Agreement that they will not attempt to teach the technique until they have completed their full course of training and received a Certificate of qualification to do so. The Agreement also provides that if, at the end of the first three months of the First Session, Mr. Alexander should consider any pupil to be unsuitable he may advise him, or her, to retire from the Training Course; in which case a proportionate amount of the Fee that has been paid for the remaining months of the Session will be refunded.

Upon successful completion of the Training Course, the Student is granted a Certificate stating that he has been trained by Mr. Alexander and is considered by him to be qualified to teach his technique. Thereafter, a number of alternatives are available to him; he may continue at 16 Ashley Place as an Assistant to Mr Alexander, under a suitable financial arrangement; or he may teach under Mr. Alexander's direction, at one of several centres to be opened in principal towns of the British Isles. There will also be vacancies, from time to time, on the Staff of the F. Matthias Alexander Trust Fund School at Penhill, Bexley, Kent. (Trustees, The Earl of Lytton and Doctor Peter Macdonald.) In addition, there is an extensive and ever-growing demand for teachers in connection with a variety of special projects and undertakings.

In the near future there will be opportunities for teachers to work in many different parts of the world. At the present time a number of